At Issue

Are Privacy Rights Being Violated?

Other Books in the At Issue Series:

At Issue

Are Privacy Rights Being Violated?

Ronald D. Lankford, Jr., Book Editor

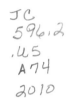

GREENHAVEN PRESS
A part of Gale, Cengage Learning

GALE
CENGAGE Learning

Detroit • New York • San Francisco • New Haven, Conn • Waterville, Maine • London

GALE
CENGAGE Learning·

Christine Nasso, *Publisher*
Elizabeth Des Chenes, *Managing Editor*

© 2010 Greenhaven Press, a part of Gale, Cengage Learning.

Gale and Greenhaven Press are registered trademarks used herein under license.

For more information, contact:
Greenhaven Press
27500 Drake Rd.
Farmington Hills, MI 48331-3535
Or you can visit our Internet site at gale.cengage.com

For product information and technology assistance, contact us at

Gale Customer Support, 1-800-877-4253
For permission to use material from this text or product, submit all requests online at
www.cengage.com/permissions

Further permissions questions can be e-mailed to permissionrequest@cengage.com

Articles in Greenhaven Press anthologies are often edited for length to meet page requirements. In addition, original titles of these works are changed to clearly present the main thesis and to explicitly indicate the author's opinion. Every effort is made to ensure that Greenhaven Press accurately reflects the original intent of the authors. Every effort has been made to trace the owners of copyrighted material.

Cover Image copyright © Images.com/Corbis.

LIBRARY OF CONGRESS CATALOGING-IN-PUBLICATION DATA

Are privacy rights being violated? / Ronald D. Lankford, Jr., book editor.
    p. cm. -- (At issue)
Includes bibliographical references and index.
ISBN 978-0-7377-4868-0 (hardcover) -- ISBN 978-0-7377-4869-7 (pbk.)
1. Privacy, Right of--United States. 2. Information technology--Social aspects--United States. 3. Information policy--United States. 4. Social norms. I. Lankford, Ronald D., 1962-
    JC596.2.U5A74 2010
    323.44'80973--dc22

2010003358

Printed in the United States of America
2 3 4 5 6   19 18 17 16 15

Contents

Introduction

Privacy rights are particularly complicated when it comes to children and health care. It is common for parents and guardians to have access to a child's medical records. Although this right is often assumed—a parent or guardian, after all, frequently oversees a child's healthcare needs—this information can become more sensitive for young adults. Can a teenager confidentially receive treatment for a sexually transmitted infection (STI)? Can a teenager confidentially visit a health care facility for contraception? Can a teenager confidentially terminate a pregnancy?

Parents are not the only ones who can legally obtain student health information. Privacy laws, as defined under the Family Educational Rights and Privacy Act (FERPA) in 1974, and as amended under the Improving America's Schools Act (IASA) in 1994, limited who had access to a minor's medical records. FERPA, however, allowed several exemptions. Medical information could be released to several organizations without parental consent, including law enforcement officials and the juvenile justice system. Medical records could also be accessed in the case of emergencies. FERPA also covers the privacy of school medical records, which are not covered in the more recent Health Insurance Portability and Accountability Act (1996). Nonetheless, it is still permissible for a teacher to share a student's school medical record with a school counselor under FERPA.

Although minors, generally speaking, have gained a greater right of privacy over the past thirty years in regard to health care, these rights are frequently provisional and also vary greatly—in the United States—from state to state.

Even with greater privacy for minors in regard to health care, complete privacy is not always guaranteed. One example of this is when a young adult seeks care or testing for an STI in the United States. All states and the District of Columbia allow minors to seek out testing and treatment without parental consent, though there are age restrictions in some states (requiring that a minor be, generally, at least twelve or fourteen before receiving treatment without parental consent). But even though minors may seek out testing without parental consent, eighteen states allow (but do not require) doctors to inform parents or guardians. In Iowa, however, state law requires the physician to notify parents if a minor tests HIV positive.

In general, minors have been allowed confidential access to contraceptive services without parental involvement. Although policies and requirements vary from state to state, overall, privacy rights relating to contraception have been supported by federal laws and by the Supreme Court. Likewise, most states support confidential prenatal care for minors. In a number of states, however, doctors can (but do not have to) inform parents that their daughter is receiving prenatal care.

Privacy in relation to abortions, however, is more limited. Although courts have allowed that parents do not have a veto power over a young adult's choice to have an abortion, the parent, in most cases, still has to be notified. In many states, a child must inform one parent of her decision to have an abortion twenty-four to forty-eight hours before the procedure. A few states require the notification of both parents; two states require no notification. A number of states waive the notification requirement in the case of abuse or neglect.

Issues revolving around privacy and minors are seldom absolute. With socially controversial issues like contraception, abortion, and drug and alcohol treatment, both state and federal legislators frequently push for greater restrictions on privacy rights for minors. Social critics and concerned parents argue that minors lack the maturity to make life-changing decisions without adult supervision. Likewise, they argue access to a child's medical history is essential because parents and guardians remain responsible for the well-being and health care of a minor.

Health officials, however, have argued that limitations on the privacy of minors are potentially harmful. Many minors, they note, begin making adult decisions during their teenage years, and they should likewise be able to make confidential decisions about health care. Along with other organizations, the Guttmacher Institute, which promotes sexual and reproductive health, argues that the general trend toward greater privacy is beneficial to the overall health of minors, stating in a report on October 1, 2009, "This trend reflects the recognition that, while parental involvement in minors' health care decisions is desirable, many minors will not avail themselves of important services if they are forced to involve their parents."

Overall, minors in the United States have a number of legal precedents that partially protect their medical privacy. The debate over the privacy of medical records and health care for minors, however, produces many strongly felt opinions and seems likely to continue into the future.

The Right of Privacy Is Destroyed by Video Cameras in Public Places

The New York Civil Liberties Union

The New York Civil Liberties Union is a branch of the American Civil Liberties Union and is dedicated to the defense of First Amendment rights.

Following 9/11, the police installed thousands of security cameras in New York city. Although proponents for cameras believe surveillance increases public safety, these cameras may also undermine the right of privacy. New technology allows a video camera to capture much more than a person committing a crime. Today's cameras are capable of identifying the print of the book or newspaper a person is reading, and a series of cameras can follow a person's movement throughout the day. Digital images are also easy to store, and with few rules or laws limiting the use of these images, they are easy to share. The New York Police Department (NYPD) has increasingly used surveillance cameras during public gatherings, a practice that potentially singles out protesters. It is incumbent upon elected officials in New York city to regulate the use of cameras in public places in order to balance issues of public safety with citizens' right of privacy.

Have you ever attended a political event? Sought treatment from a psychiatrist? Had a drink at a gay bar? Visited a fertility clinic? Met a friend for a private conversation?

Who's Watching?. New York: The New York Civil Liberties Union, 2006. Reproduced by permission.

Might you have felt differently about engaging in such activities had you known that you could be videotaped in the act—and that there would be no rules governing the distribution of what had been recorded?

The Law Is Not Keeping Up with the Growing Number of Cameras

The fact is, conduct most of us think of as private and anonymous is increasingly taking place under the electronic gaze of video surveillance cameras. Since 9/11, the number of surveillance cameras in New York City has skyrocketed. And our lawmakers have failed to keep up: video surveillance cameras can be operated with almost no legal constraint or consequence.

Proponents of video surveillance cameras advocate that the city dedicate significant amounts of tax dollars to maintaining a video surveillance network. Cameras, they contend, enhance public safety by deterring crime. But while video images may assist in criminal investigations after the fact, there is a dearth of evidence that supports the contention that video surveillance cameras actually prevent or deter crime.

There is, however, a growing body of evidence that indicates the proliferation of video surveillance technology is undermining fundamental rights of privacy, speech, expression, and association. Troubling examples of that evidence come from the video archives of the New York Police Department [NYPD].

This report seeks to generate a discussion about the critical questions that have yet to be asked by city officials regarding the rapidly growing number of surveillance cameras: What objectives are served by the use of video surveillance technology? What rules and guidelines are needed regarding the retention and transfer of video images? What constraints should be placed upon the government's access to video images produced by private entities? What remedies will be available to an injured party when prohibitions on the operation of video surveillance cameras are violated? . . .

Vanishing Privacy Rights in a Technological Age

Today's surveillance camera is not merely the equivalent of a pair of eyes. It has super-human vision. It has the capability to zoom in and "read" the pages of the book you have opened while waiting for a train in the subway. What's more, this camera can tilt, pan, and rotate—making it increasingly easy to track you as you move through your day. Facial recognition software, while still imperfect, will someday be able to capture your image from the faces in a crowd, and then compare the image of your face against the facial images stored in a law-enforcement database.

Cumbersome video tapes have morphed into digital images that can be inexpensively stored en masse *on computers indefinitely.*

And cameras are ubiquitous. A *New York Post* reporter once gathered images from the 200-plus security cameras (both private and government) he passed on a normal Tuesday on the job. At 9:51 a.m. he was caught on film buying coffee at a deli near his Brooklyn apartment. About an hour later, he was captured driving on the Brooklyn Queens Expressway by a Department of Transportation traffic camera. From there he was spotted entering the *Post*'s offices on Sixth Avenue and Forty-eighth Street, and riding the elevator to his office. Later that day he was filmed talking to a source while eating lunch in Times Square, taking the subway, having a drink with a friend at a café in Greenwich Village, and renting a DVD on Court Street back in Brooklyn.

Moreover, rapid advances in technology have made the broad dissemination of video images a simple matter. In other words, the recording of a single videotaped incident may well involve more than a single observation of your conduct and whereabouts. Once the recorded image exists, whether in digital or videotape format, it can be scrutinized over and over again by anyone to whom access is made possible.

Cumbersome video tapes have morphed into digital images that can be inexpensively stored *en masse* on computers indefinitely. Massive amounts of information in computer memory banks can be searched and shared with the click of a mouse. Universal access to stored video images can occur in a matter of seconds.

Some security advocates see every advance in video surveillance technology as an enhancement of public safety. But even with clear rules and procedures in place, horrendous privacy violations can and do occur. It was revealed several years ago that the State of Florida had been selling photographic images and other personal information stored on driver's licenses to commercial marketers. The state and its private-sector partners undertook this venture without notice to the public.

Mission creep—the expansion of a project or mission beyond its original goals—is well-documented in the government's handling of sensitive personal information. History has shown that databases created for one purpose are almost inevitably used for other, not always legitimate, purposes. In the absence of legal constraints, the illicit purposes for which video images may be used are limited only by the imagination. Police officials could create a video archive of anti-war protestors. An NYPD video unit might target black or Latino youth who enter a majority-white neighborhood. A security professional could use video records to stalk someone. As one Fourth Amendment scholar has pointed out:

> A detective or spy wishing to build a dossier on an individual's life and personality would probably learn more from examining a searchable database of such images than

he would by rummaging through a purse, wallet, or suitcase, especially if he could link from the images to other information about the individual's identity and background.

Threats to Freedom of Speech and Association

In recent years the NYPD has been arming special police units with state-of-the-art video surveillance cameras. This innovation in police tactics represents another setback for the First Amendment.

New York City has a long and troubled history of police surveillance of individuals and groups engaged in lawful political protest and dissent. Between 1904 and 1985 the NYPD compiled some one million intelligence files on more than 200,000 individuals and groups—suspected communists, Vietnam War protesters, health and housing advocates, education reform groups, and civil rights activists.

It wasn't until 1985, after more than a decade of litigation, that the New York Police Department's Security and Investigation Section (otherwise known as the Red Squad) was finally reined in by a federal judge. That class-action lawsuit led to the Handschu Agreement, which prohibited the police department from "commencing an investigation" into the political, ideological or religious activities of an individual or group unless the department had "specific information . . . that a person or group engaged in political activity is engaged in, about to engage in or has threatened to engage in conduct which constitutes a crime. . . ."

But in 2003 the court significantly modified the Handschu Agreement, providing the police with far greater latitude to undertake surveillance of individuals involved in political activity. The latitude afforded by this new standard is required, the NYPD argued, in light of the heightened threat of terrorism. Under the new guidelines the police can undertake a preliminary inquiry based upon "information indicating the possibility of criminal activity."

The Republican National Convention

The court's relaxation of the Handschu Agreement makes far more vulnerable the First Amendment rights of speech, expression, and association. This became obvious during the 2004 Republican National Convention [RNC] in New York City, when the NYPD placed demonstrators under an electronic dragnet. Hundreds of thousands of people participated in protests, including a huge anti-war demonstration on the day before the convention began. Despite predictions from law enforcement authorities that the convention might be the target of violence or even terrorism, the demonstrations were nonviolent except for several isolated incidents. . . .

The NYPD retained hundreds if not thousands of hours of surveillance images captured during the policing of the RNC, some of which were published by the *New York Times* as "an unofficial archive of police videotapes" four months after the convention. The archives clearly include conduct that has nothing to do with a crime. And some of that conduct is of a personal and highly sensitive nature. One of the police department images published by the *Times*, for example, showed a couple in an intimate embrace on a rooftop terrace.

There is only limited recognition in the law that there are some places into which a surveillance camera is not allowed to intrude.

Why did the police videotape this couple? Why was the image retained? How many images of this nature are stored in the police department's archives? There are no reliable answers to these questions. The lack of answers indicates that serious invasions of personal privacy are inevitable because of the city's failure to regulate video surveillance technology.

The [New York Civil Liberties Union] NYCLU is back in court, challenging the NYPD's practice of collecting and archiving video images of people engaged in constitutionally protected speech and expression. However the court may rule, it can be expected that the police will continue to push the envelope in an effort to monitor political dissent. Thousands of video cameras now stationed throughout the city record the activities of political protesters who happen to be within camera range. Police armed with handheld cameras capture thousands of video "close-ups" in the streets. If the NYPD retains these digital images, they will serve as a permanent, "searchable" archive—in essence, visual dossiers on dissenters. . . .

Privacy Rights in Danger

There is only limited recognition in the law that there are some places into which a surveillance camera is not allowed to intrude. And there are virtually no rules that prohibit police or private entities from archiving, selling, or freely transmitting images captured by a video surveillance camera. The courts have yet to address the fundamental privacy and associational rights implicated by the phenomenon of widespread video surveillance. Philadelphia Police Inspector Thomas Nestel, author of a widely cited study on video surveillance, has warned that "forging ahead with reckless abandon by providing no written direction, no supervision, no training and no regulating legislation creates a recipe for disaster."

The findings documented in this report indicate the nature and magnitude of the harm posed by the unregulated proliferation of video surveillance cameras. It is now incumbent upon the [New York] City Council and Mayor Michael Bloomberg to address this issue with the seriousness it requires. New York City must enact comprehensive, well-crafted legislation that recognizes video surveillance technology affects fundamental rights and liberties, and that the use of such technology must reasonably balance the city's interest in protecting public safety with the individual's interest in enjoying personal privacy.

2

Video Cameras Help Protect the Public from Police Abuse

Katherine Mangu-Ward

Katherine Mangu-Ward is a senior editor at Reason *magazine.*

While it is worthwhile that organizations like the New York Civil Liberties Union (NYCLU) recognize the right of privacy in public spaces, people should also understand the benefits of surveillance cameras. Surveillance cameras may diminish privacy, but they also render public spaces transparent. For instance, cameras help provide general security, and they also protect citizens from police misbehavior. Further, the private movement and behavior of most people can already be traced through credit cards, transportation passes, and ATM transactions. Perhaps the greatest concern in regard to loss of privacy is police surveillance and the potential misuse of video information, even though most abuses of stored images have been relatively minor. The use of cameras by police departments also has an added benefit: Police officers who know they are being watched by a camera will be less likely to use unnecessary force. The loss of privacy is an important issue to debate, but the NYCLU's concern that government cameras will further erode these rights ignores the benefits these cameras bring to public safety.

"Have you ever attended a political event? Sought treatment from a psychiatrist? Had a drink at a gay bar? Visited a fertility clinic?" A report on the proliferation of sur-

Katherine Mangu-Ward, "Is Privacy Overrated?" *Reason*, January 9, 2007. Copyright © 2007 by Reason Foundation, 3415 S. Sepulveda Blvd., Suite 400, Los Angeles, CA 90034, www.reason.com. Reproduced by permission.

veillance cameras—more than 4,200 below 14th street [in New York city]—from the New York Civil Liberties Union [NYCLU] asks: Would you have done those things if you had known you were being watched?

The answer, for most people, is yes. Though we may shy away from the idea of someone spying on our private lives, most people believe that we live in a country where rights are generally respected, and so we go about our business without fear. However, the report notes:

> There is only limited recognition in the law that there are some places into which a surveillance camera is not allowed to intrude. And there are virtually no rules that prohibit police or private entities from archiving, selling or freely transmitting images captured by a video surveillance camera. The courts have yet to address the fundamental privacy and associational rights implicated by the phenomenon of widespread video surveillance.

In short, they're worried about what will happen when New Yorkers no longer have an expectation of some degree of privacy in the public sphere. And they're right: There is almost no privacy left in America, especially in cities. Sooner or later, you won't be able to go anywhere without being tracked.

Surveillance Benefits

Debate about the use and abuse of surveillance cameras is worthwhile, but it is also worth keeping in mind the ways in which we benefit from the death-by-a-thousand-cuts that privacy suffers every day. While raising legitimate concerns about the camera boom in New York, the report ignores the significant gains to consumers living in a transparent society—both convenience and security—and the ways in which proliferation of video surveillance public and private can protect citizens from police misbehavior or other miscarriages of justice.

Let's revisit the frightening picture painted by the New York Civil Liberties Union. For a session at the psychiatrist's office or the fertility clinic, you would have paid with a credit card, right? If you bought a round of drinks at the gay bar, would you have hesitated to hand your card to the bartender, even to leave it with him to run a tab? To get there, you might have taken the subway using your registered, traceable Metro card. Or perhaps you drove, zipping past tollbooths in an EZ Pass lane [which lets prepaid drivers avoid stopping to pay tolls], pitying the poor suckers waiting to pay with old-fashioned, anonymous cash. If you were concerned about getting lost, you could have used your phone's GPS, leaving a wake of signals and records about your location and habits.

Perhaps you would have stopped to pick up some cash at an ATM before your outing. There, you would have created another digital record, stamped with the time and place of your withdrawal in the bank's records. And that mirror above the ATM where you checked out your hair? It's concealing a camera, there to protect you from anyone inspired to lift your newly acquired cash or force you to take out more at gunpoint, or at least help identify and catch the mugger later. ATM cameras have been in general use for many years.

Your credit card, EZ Pass, and bank records can all be subpoenaed when necessary. So, do a few thousand city cameras really represent a new invasion of our privacy? Hardly. My credit card company has long known where I buy underwear, but I don't lay awake nights worried that prosecutors might demand knowledge of my preferences in skivvies. The ways in which that information can be accessed by the state are circumscribed by decades of legal precedent. We should remain vigilant that those precedents aren't eroded, and we should work to strengthen protections where necessary, but the collection of the information in itself is an unstoppable force, mostly for good—I *like* that I can sift through records of everything I have purchased in the last three years.

New York already boasts three or four thousand cameras, mostly private, and the number will only continue to grow.

The biggest boom will be in government cameras, though. The New York City police recently announced plans to create "a citywide system of closed-circuit televisions" operated from a central control center, funded primarily by federal anti-terrorism money.

Added surveillance of police also carries another benefit: Police are smart enough to know to be careful when they are being taped.

Admittedly, this is where the surveillance nation gets dicey. Concerns about misuse of public cameras by authorities are reasonable, and violations should be punished—there are several cases wending their way through the courts now which are expected to set standards for how severely abuse of video can be punished, and what the proper parameters are for its use. But much of the abuse of the cameras often takes innocuous forms: a deputy police commissioner rewinding tape to locate his lost keys or keeping an eye on his kids as they walk home from school. This type of behavior should not be confused with serious infractions.

And, of course, cameras can and should also protect citizens from police misbehavior. Several protesters at the 2004 Republican convention in New York, for example, have beaten charges of resisting arrest with video evidence from private and public cameras. A few more cameras on the street when police fired 50 rounds at Sean Bell in Queens might have helped determine what really happened on the night of November 25th [a 2006 incident that sparked criticism of the local police].

There have been several smaller occasions where do-it-yourself video privacy violations have paid off, as in the case of recent LAPD [Los Angeles Police Department] brutality caught on a mobile phone or handheld camera. Think Rodney King meets YouTube. In these cases, private cameras provided a check on police. Added surveillance of police also carries another benefit: Police are smart enough to know to be careful when they are being taped, even when they're being taped by their own colleagues. The report relates an interview with off-duty police officers at a labor demonstration. "A special NYPD [New York Police Department] unit was assigned to film the police officers as they demonstrated. 'That's Big Brother watching you,' said one police demonstrator outside Gracie Mansion [home to New York's mayor]. Said another: 'Sends a chill down a police officer's back to think that Internal Affairs would be taping something.'"

Police concerned about who's watching them will generally be police more prone to good behavior.

Surveillance and Crime

More worrying than the boom in public cameras, though, is a recent proposal to require New York's hundreds of nightclubs to install cameras on the premises. When businesses choose to install cameras for their own purposes, the cameras usually benefit consumers in the long run—with increased security or convenience. But when the city mandates the installation of private cameras, patrons are less likely to benefit. Such mandates can and should be fought as infringements on privacy and property.

Whether . . . cameras deter illegal behavior is a legitimate debate, and it's true that cameras in the London subways system didn't deter bombers in July 2005. But perhaps it should have—the video footage led to the speedy identification and capture of the four bombers. The next terrorists (those not hoping for 72 virgins, anyway) might be inclinded to rethink their plans.

If you're inclined to avoid the cameras, go ahead. . . . The NYCLU report is concerned that the cameras are often disguised, that they "remain hidden to the untrained eye." But in the same sentence, the report notes that "the corner deli" or other shopkeepers often operate cameras. Small shopkeepers have been using security cameras for many years, but even the most paranoid among us still go in to pick up some beef jerky when we pay for our gas. Our behavior suggests that we are already at peace with having our images captured on video.

Of course, issues like required surveillance on private property and protections for citizens who want to film police should be aired in the public square. Police occasionally arrest bystanders for taping a police encounter, an activity that should clearly be protected. But the debate shouldn't ignore the fact that the kind of personal privacy many worry about losing to street-corner cameras has already mostly been lost to credit cards, EZ Passes, and cameras in your ATM or deli. And more cameras and records, not fewer, may be the best guarantee against abuse of police power in the age of zero privacy.

3

The U.S. Government Does Offer Protection Against Identity Theft

The President's Identity Theft Task Force

The President's Identity Theft Task Force was commissioned by President George W. Bush in 2006 to develop a national strategy in relation to identity theft.

The Identity Theft Task Force was commissioned by President George W. Bush in 2006 to develop a national strategy in relation to identity theft. The task force's issued report focused on recommendations in four key areas: to initiate new procedures for public and private institutions that will protect consumer data from criminals, to develop strategies that will make it more difficult for thieves to misuse consumer data, to assist consumers who have suffered from identity theft, and to prosecute and punish those who commit identity theft crimes. While each of these key areas will help address the issue of identity theft, there are no easy solutions. Because the methods and techniques of criminals continue to evolve and change, protecting consumers from identity theft will require continued vigilance.

Two years ago [in 2006], the President [George W. Bush] launched a new era in the fight against identity theft by issuing an executive order establishing the Identity Theft Task Force. The executive order charged 15 federal departments and agencies with crafting a comprehensive national strategy

"Introduction, Conclusion," The President's Identity Theft Task Force Report, September 2008, pp. vii–viii, 50. IDTheft.gov.

to combat more effectively this pernicious crime, which afflicts millions of Americans each year and, in some cases, causes devastating damage to its victims. One year later, on April 11, 2007, the Task Force submitted its Strategic Plan to the President. The Strategic Plan examined the nature and scope of identity theft and offered a far-reaching series of recommendations to reduce its incidence and impact. Although these recommendations were directed primarily at improving the federal government's response to identity theft, the Task Force recognized that everyone—consumers, the private sector, and federal, state, and local governments—has a role to play in fighting this crime.

This report documents the Task Force's efforts to implement the Strategic Plan's recommendations. The Task Force has successfully carried out most of the recommendations or is making substantial progress in doing so.

The Strategic Plan included recommendations in four key areas:

- *Data protection*—keeping consumer data out of the hands of criminals

- *Avoiding data misuse*—making it harder for criminals to exploit consumer data

- *Victim assistance*—making it easier for victims to detect and recover from identity theft . . .

- *Deterrence*—increasing prosecution and punishment of perpetrators

In these four areas, the Task Force made a total of 31 recommendations, ranging from small, incremental steps to broad policy changes.

The Four Task Areas

First, with respect to data protection, the Task Force has promoted a new culture of security in the public and private sectors. For the public sector, the Task Force member agencies launched a variety of initiatives aimed at making the federal government a better custodian of sensitive personal information. The Office of Management and Budget, for example, worked to educate all federal agencies on improving data security practices and is monitoring their performance in doing so. The Office of Personnel Management led an inter-agency initiative to eliminate unnecessary uses of Social Security numbers (SSNs)—one of the most valuable commodities for identity thieves—in federal government human resource functions, while individual agencies began to eliminate unnecessary uses of SSNs in other aspects of their work.

The Task Force encouraged similar data security efforts in the private sector by launching several policymaking, outreach, and enforcement initiatives.

The Task Force expanded its data security and identity theft business and consumer education campaigns through speeches, videos, articles, brochures, testimony, interviews, tip sheets, and a best practices workshop for businesses. In one important example, the U.S. Postal Service delivered a mailing in early 2008 to 146 million U.S. residences and businesses with advice on how to protect themselves against identity theft. Task Force member agencies continued to investigate and, where appropriate, take civil, administrative, or criminal enforcement action against individuals and entities for violations of data security laws and regulations.

Second, the Task Force examined ways to prevent identity theft by making it harder for thieves to misuse consumer data. Member agencies held two public workshops that explored means of improving consumer authentication processes to prevent thieves from using stolen personal information to access existing accounts or open new ones. One of the workshops specifically addressed the availability and use of SSNs in the authentication process, and whether there are better and less sensitive substitutes. These workshops provided opportunities for public and private sector representatives and consumer advocates to explore these issues.

Third, the Task Force launched a number of initiatives to assist identity theft victims when they begin the sometimes arduous task of repairing their credit and restoring their good names. Task Force member agencies over the past year provided identity theft training to over 900 law enforcement officers—often the first sources to whom victims turn—from over 250 agencies. Task Force members also trained victim assistance counselors and provided grants to organizations that directly help identity theft victims. Task Force members developed and posted an Identity Theft Victim Statement of Rights and are working closely with the American Bar Association on a pro bono legal assistance program for identity theft victims. Task Force members also are continuing to evaluate the effectiveness of various laws and programs designed to help victims, such as state identity theft "passport" programs, state credit freeze laws, and rights granted under the Fair and Accurate Credit Transactions Act of 2003.

What makes identity theft especially challenging is its dynamic and rapidly changing nature.

Fourth, the Task Force worked to improve law enforcement's ability to investigate, prosecute, and punish identity thieves by proposing legislation to Congress, improving coordination and training for local law enforcers, and targeting criminal enforcement initiatives. Task Force members also are enhancing international cooperation by partnering with foreign law enforcement agencies in identity theft investigations and providing them with training and assistance, and encouraging greater information sharing among and between law enforcement agencies and the private sector.

No Simple Solutions

The Task Force's Strategic Plan notes that there is no simple solution to identity theft. It is an ever-evolving problem with many dimensions. Public concerns about the security of personal information and identity theft remain at high levels, with potentially serious consequences for the functioning of our economy. The efforts of the Task Force over the past year to implement the Plan's recommendations have underscored the need for a comprehensive and coordinated response from both the public and private sectors. These efforts have already made a difference and will continue to do so in the coming years.

The battle against identity theft is a shared responsibility. Consumers, businesses, and other organizations that collect consumer data; information technology and software providers that supply anti-fraud solutions; and federal, state, and local governments are all impacted by identity theft and have roles to play in the fight against it.

> *Government and the private sector, working together with consumers, must remain vigilant, adaptable, and nimble as new generations of identity thieves and techniques develop over the coming years.*

What makes identity theft especially challenging is its dynamic and rapidly changing nature. The profiles, purposes, and methods of the perpetrators are continually changing. Identity theft today can be the product of organized crime rings here and abroad using increasingly sophisticated technologies, such as installing malicious software, phishing, spoofing, and database hacking, to tap into repositories of consumer data. Increasingly, criminals combine these techniques for better effect, many of which are facilitated by commercially available tools. At the same time, the more traditional "low tech" methods of stealing identities—insider breaches, dumpster diving, garden variety purse snatching, and the like—continue.

Preventing Identity Theft

The fight against identity theft is an "end to end" challenge in which the security risks and responsibilities are spread from consumers, to enterprises, to information technology and telecommunication vendors, software providers, and others who facilitate the collection, use, maintenance, and eventual destruction of personal information. Newer areas of identity theft are growing fast, as thieves steal data in order to commit medical, immigration, employment, and mortgage fraud, for example. What identity theft will look like ten years from now is impossible to predict.

In April 2007, the Task Force released a plan for attacking identity theft that relies on the contributions of all stakeholders, working in cooperation. The Strategic Plan recommends the use of all available tools, from enhanced consumer and business education, to better data security and consumer authentication, to expanded resources for victim recovery, to increased training and support for our foreign law enforcement partners, to more certain and stronger punishment for perpetrators.

Over the past year or so, the Task Force members have worked to implement the recommendations of the Strategic Plan. Much of this work has been completed; some is ongoing. Many in the private and not-for-profit sectors also have taken important steps to reduce the incidence of identity theft. The fight against identity theft will not end when we have implemented the 31 recommendations in the Plan, however. Identity theft must be treated aggressively, yet with the recognition that it is an ongoing and evolving problem, that there is no "silver bullet" that will end it, and that its perpetrators will be ever more creative. Government and the private sector, working together with consumers, must remain vigilant, adaptable, and nimble as new generations of identity thieves and techniques develop over the coming years.

Internet Data-Mining Violates Privacy Rights

John C. Dvorak

John C. Dvorak hosts an Internet television program titled Dvorak Live on the Web.

Companies obtain "deep information" on a person through e-mail accounts, information on the products she likes/dislikes, and information on her personal habits, and they use that information to attempt to sell products to her. Internet concerns such as Google collect this kind of information each time an individual uses the company's search engines and e-mail. "Tweets" may provide even more deep information on consumers in the future. Unfortunately, access to this information, especially when sold to other companies, has the potential to become exploitive.

As you read this column, someone somewhere is probably lurking in your life, plowing through everything you do online to try to learn more about you. And while there are plenty of reasons why a person might want to do this, here's the most likely one: He or she is finding a way to rob you blind by selling you lots of stuff you probably don't need. Why do you acquiesce? Because this person knows your hot buttons well.

Deep information about individuals has always been the holy grail of marketers. If I know everything about your tastes, likes and dislikes, attitudes, and even casual thoughts, I'll bet I can find something you want to buy, and persuade you to buy it from me.

John C. Dvorak, "Data Mining and the Death of Privacy," www.pcmag.com, vol. 28, May 1, 2009, pp. 38–39. Copyright © 2009 Ziff Davis Publishing Holdings Inc. All rights reserved. Reprinted with permission.

Google and Privacy

Google is now the most dangerous company in the world, not only because it constantly acquires this deep information, but because it keeps striving to do it better and better. Recently I was in my Google e-mail account and found a peculiar message: "Lots of space—over 7313.643755 megabytes (and counting) of free storage so you'll never need to delete another message." The last time I was paying attention I had a gigabyte and then maybe two. Now 7 and growing? And why is Google encouraging me to save all my e-mail on its servers? Because it's data mining me.

If it can be monitored, it can be exploited. If it can be exploited, then something can be sold.

I don't keep my e-mail on Google but on the server of a friend of mine, so I don't have to worry about being data mined. But imagine the weird stuff you could find out about me if you had access to the 61,000 messages in the inbox, and 30,000 in the outbox!

Does anyone feel uncomfortable about any of this? You can easily profile someone with this many messages; you can find out his or her political leanings, love affairs, bad habits, banking information, you name it.

Now I would hate to accuse Google of doing anything nefarious, but let's face it, Google is more of a marketing technology company than anything else. And this brings us to Blogger and Twitter. If you think going through scads of e-mail is a data-mining bonanza, imagine going through every thought and action and (gasp!) tweet.

Data Mining

Lots of people tweet about what they're doing minute by minute. But the real gold mine for marketers—and the reason it seems obvious Google will, or should, buy Twitter—is the links. People are constantly posting links on Twitter, and they're turned into Tiny URLs that can easily be tracked. So if something is causing a buzz, it can be monitored. And if it can be monitored, it can be exploited. If it can be exploited, then something can be sold. A product can be marketed using the information.

At some point we have to say: "Google, stop already!"

It won't matter. Google has your search information; all the searches you've ever done are documented. It has all the e-mails you've written, and all your tweets are next. Not to mention your blog posts, spreadsheets, and who knows what else. No wonder the company's motto is "Don't be evil." Because the potential is certainly there.

Advertising and Data Mining

Now I believe that Google does not want to be evil with all this data. It wants to sell advertising. Let's face it, who needs the aggravation of finding a way to exploit every little step you take? What difference does it make to Google whether you are pro-life or a vegan or a member of the alliance to save the red-crested hornbeam? There is some sales angle, yes, but nothing sinister, right?

Well, not on the part of Google. But what about others who may eventually get access to this treasure trove of data? What about a political party that wants to monitor the "enemy"? You have noticed that since the days of [President] Dick Nixon the word "enemy" is used openly to describe the people who do not support the party in power, right? This is a term I do not take lightly. It's loaded and betrays the mindset of the person using the term. It's not good.

The point is obvious. Data mining is too powerful to be left to good old-fashioned advertising. I can imagine using it to determine what stock is going to skyrocket by extracting inside information. Blackmail is not out of the question, although collecting the right data might take some seriously interesting algorithms. Of course there is just plain old snooping. How would you like access to all the world's e-mail? What fun.

No matter how you cut this pie, what is going on can't end in any positive way. If Google buys Twitter, as everyone is saying it will, the motive has to be more data mining on top of what is already going on. And it would be a signal that the final nail is in the privacy coffin. Have a nice day.

5

Privacy Rights on the Internet Are Overrated

Chris Marriott

Chris Marriott is the vice president and global managing director of Acxiom Digital.

Although many people have expressed concern over privacy on the Internet, this attitude is changing with some Internet users. Not only are they comfortable sharing private information on Facebook, they appreciate the personalized experience they receive as a result. It may be possible, in the future, to create a similar, more personal experience between consumers and companies. As long as companies seek the consumer's consent first. It is also likely that more people will learn to trust favored companies with private information.

One of the classic and oft-repeated scenes in the hit series *Cheers* centered around the character Norm walking into the bar. When he entered, everyone in the bar would call out, "Norm!" With a wave of the hand, he would acknowledge them and retreat to his usual place at the bar, his beer usually poured and ready for him. Norm didn't find it creepy that everyone knew his name. Nor did he find it creepy that Sam and Coach knew exactly what he wanted before he asked. In fact, he probably would have found it quite odd if people didn't greet him and Coach didn't have his beer waiting.

Chris Marriott, "Privacy: It's Overrated," *iMedia Connection*, December 8, 2008. Reproduced by permission.

In a sense, *Cheers* was a perfect example of customer recognition and the ability to anticipate that customer's needs at the exact right time. And as a result, Norm was a very valuable repeat customer.

When Norm finally got home from the bar at night—if we fast-forwarded the show's backdrop to within the last several years—he would have found numerous credit card solicitations in his mailbox addressed to him, Norm Peterson, at his home address. Now Norm would have been a little foggy from the numerous beers, so he probably didn't take at face value comments like, "Due to your superior credit history, we are able to offer you. ..." Little did he know that the card issuer actually *did* know his complete credit history and score and *did* make that offer specifically to him (and people like him). That might have creeped him out a little. But the fact that the sender knew that Norm Peterson lived at that exact address wouldn't even cross Norm's mind as an issue of concern.

The key difference lies in the internet itself. From its infancy, the internet has sat at a nexus of anonymity and vulnerability.

And if the phone then rang (because Norm was not on the do-not-call registry yet), and the same company made him an offer, he would not have thought twice about the fact that the company had *his* phone number as well as his address—though he might have been irked by the intrusion. Norm expected to be recognized in places where he was a customer, and wasn't bothered by the fact that companies with whom he didn't do business knew who he was, his phone number and where he lived.

The Internet and Personal Information

So why all the angst today around using customer recognition tools to welcome returnees to your site? Why are people concerned that companies are using data gathered from how they got there, what they did with you previously and personal data that you've been able to append to their other data?

The key difference lies in the internet itself. From its infancy, the internet has sat at a nexus of anonymity and vulnerability. The web in particular allowed people to investigate all kinds of things without letting other people know, from porn to new jobs. But at the same time, the internet brought with it a sense that nefarious types could take advantage of anonymity to rip people off. Countless scams, phishing and security breaches have taught consumers fear.

This situation will not persist forever, though. For a glimpse of the future, take a look at how young adults use Facebook. These users spend hours customizing their Facebook pages, writing on friends' walls and adding status updates. They post photos and videos. Why? Because sharing all of this personal information leads to a better Facebook experience. It helps them connect better with friends and be the life of the party.

As these adults get older (and as more old fogies invade Facebook), users will demand the opportunity to trade personal information for a more involving experience from brands they like and trust. A childless user will become frustrated when, for instance, a retailer shows her baby clothing on the site homepage. A mom with three kids will roll her eyes when an auto manufacturer's site puts a sports car on the homepage.

A Personalized Web Experience

The transition will not happen overnight, nor will marketers find it an easy task at first. Facebook succeeds because it asks for information in an incremental way—members can give as much information as they wish. Marketers will need to find relevant ways to address the situation.

For instance, a marketer could start by establishing a baseline of personalization behavior. Using cookies, the marketer could simply greet identified users with a personal note at the top of the homepage ("Welcome back, Norm"). Many sites already take this step. However, the marketer should also give the user the opportunity to browse anonymously by providing an appropriate link next to the greeting ("Let me browse anonymously").

To be successful, personalization has to start basic and with user consent.

For visitors who do not reject the greeting, take the next step. When the identified user visits the next time, place a banner or link that invites him or her to see a personalized version of the site. Clicking on the link reveals a version of the same page personalized according to one or two basic variables, such as gender or purchase history. This page should also explain why the page is different and give the user the option to see personalized versions of the site from then on.

As the users become more accustomed to the personalized site, the site owner can add increasingly sophisticated takes on personalization. But to be successful, personalization has to start basic and with user consent. While consumers will someday expect this kind of treatment, they do not expect it yet. But the key is to not let your fear of the issue of consumer privacy keep you from actually doing things that Norm (or your customers) would appreciate, now and in the future.

Marketers who don't make efforts to recognize their best customers in all channels may meet with a fate best described by Norm himself: "It's a dog-eat-dog world, and I'm wearing Milk-Bone underwear."

6

National ID Cards Do Violate Privacy Rights

Neil Richard Leslie

Neil Richard Leslie is an assistant editor at the Atlantic Council.

While many of the countries that have suffered from terrorist attacks have issued national ID cards, Britain and the United States have been—until now—exceptions. Even as both governments have announced plans to issue national IDs, however, the public has been—with good reason—hesitant. Britain decided to begin issuing national IDs in November of 2008, first to foreign nationals and later to British citizens. While the national IDs have not initially been required, protest groups like No2ID (No to ID) believe that the British government will eventually require the card for all citizens. The United States may take a similar path. The cost of initiating the program in both countries is prohibitive, $30 billion in the U.K. and $17 billion in the United States, and the ID cards will be incapable of accomplishing their initially stated purpose: to reduce terrorism. Also, national IDs are seen by civil liberty groups as a threat to privacy. Whereas certain technologies like data mining target specific individuals, national IDs monitor everyone. ID technology has proved accessible to criminals, and many citizens do not trust the government to keep personal information secure. Terrorism will continue to be a problem; giving up the right of privacy will not solve it.

Neil Richard Leslie, "Privacy, Biometrics and the War on Terror," *New Atlanticist*, October 8, 2008. Reproduced by permission.

Anglo-Americans are the exception when it comes to national ID cards. Almost every other major country that has suffered from terrorism in the past quarter-century has instituted some form of compulsory national identification. Germany, Spain, Israel, Turkey, Russia, China, Saudi Arabia, Egypt and Pakistan have all done so. The United States and the United Kingdom on the other hand share in their deficiency with countries such as Iraq, Afghanistan, Yemen and Sri Lanka.

An Attack on Privacy

As argued below, there is good reason that the Anglo-American public is resistant to national identification cards. Yet the British and American governments seem increasingly willing to neglect privacy in pursuit of personal data.

As unveiled last month [September 2008], the United Kingdom [U.K.] will start issuing national ID cards beginning in November. Initially, the card will be necessary only for foreign nationals, but will later be offered to the wider population pending legislation making it a legal requirement for all British citizens. Although the government emphasizes the voluntary aspect of the scheme and talks of a "consumer-led" shift to ID cards—citing the alleged benefits of reduced identity theft and increased security—the whole venture will be rendered useless unless compulsion is enforced. Indeed, what would be the benefit in terms of national security if a significant number of the population could opt out of having an ID card? And if one can prove who they are to get an ID card in the first place, then why do they need one? Some groups, such as No2ID, see this initial phase as the thin end of a wedge, "a softening-up exercise" for the introduction of identity cards for everyone. The government, aware of the meager public sentiment for foreign immigrants, is exploiting the weakness of this disenfranchised group, using [its members] as guinea pigs for the wider roll-out expected in 2011.

The U.S. equivalent to Britain's legislation is the Real ID Act of 2005, which Republican Ron Paul has warned "establishes a national ID card" and "gives authority to the Secretary of Homeland Security to unilaterally add requirements as he sees fit." Currently the American scheme is a little less defined, yet public opinion in both countries towards these bills is skeptical. In Europe, however, where ID cards are already widely used, they tend to be looked upon more favorably. They double as passports between EU [European Union] countries; they save time and energy by combining multiple documents on one small card, and they ensure that critical information is available to doctors in the event of an emergency should a patient's medical record be unavailable. Why then are the Anglo-Americans so averse to these proposals?

Civil liberty groups understandably decry the introduction of ID cards as an attack on personal privacy.

The fundamental flaw with ID cards, aside from the financial cost (an estimated $30 billion in the U.K. over the next ten years, and $17 billion in the U.S.), is that it will not prevent terrorism, nor even significantly reduce it. Even the former British Home Secretary admitted this much. ID cards, mandatory in Spain, did not prevent the murder of 191 innocent people in the Madrid bombings. Some of the attackers even possessed valid IDs. True, it made it easier for the *guardias civiles* to find and track down the culprits after the attack, but those terrorists who seek to destroy our way of life care neither about being killed nor [being] captured. No matter how advanced the biometric technology, nor how stringent the implementation of the cards, the efficacy of such a scheme will be undermined unless neighboring countries possess an equally efficient system. Otherwise, potential terrorists could enter a "soft" state and obtain a valid ID there before travelling on to their target country. And that is not to mention home-grown terrorists such as those responsible for the London bombings. How do ID cards guard against disillusioned Muslims accessing an Islamist website exhorting them to blow up fellow citizens?

Civil liberty groups understandably decry the introduction of ID cards as an attack on personal privacy. Under the U.K. scheme, information will be recorded on a central National Identity Register (NIR), where data such as gender, fingerprints, iris scans and 47 other identificatory categories can be legally recorded. What is to stop one of the individuals operating this database from being blackmailed into forging an ID for use by a criminal gang or terrorist cell? Britain is already one the most heavily surveilled nations on earth. For a country that constitutes one percent of the global population, the U.K. is home to twenty percent of the world's CCTV [closed-circuit television] cameras.

> *When we give up our right to privacy, we are not only giving up our rights, but the rights of future generations.*

Imperfect Technology

A more effective tool for preventing terrorist attacks, but no less controversial, is a method known as "data mining," whereby suspicious electronic patterns of behaviour are tracked and recorded. In the U.S., computer-driven searches look through an individual's web history, credit card transactions and personal background, allowing authorities to flag suspect behaviour. *The Economist* offers the example of a Muslim chemistry graduate who takes an ill-paid job at a farm-supplies store. What does this signify? Is he merely earning some cash, or using the job as cover to get his hands on a supply of potassium nitrate (used in fertiliser, and explosives)? What if his credit-card records show purchases of timing devices? Data mining allows analysts this information, but it is left to their judgement to decide whether or not it constitutes the beginnings of a criminal plot, or just some innocent individual's "eccentric but legal behaviour." If data mining can detect suspect patterns, then ID cards have nothing to offer in their own right. Data mining monitors suspicious behaviour; ID cards monitor us all.

There are also failings with the technology. The new Radio Frequency [Identification] (RFID) technology found in some passports has already been hacked by illegal scanners at 30 paces. It is not inconceivable that these scanners could be acquired by terrorist groups or criminal gangs. Furthermore, public confidence in the British government's ability to store their private information securely was shattered last year when a civil servant working for H.M. [Her Majesty's, a reference to Britain's monarch] Customs lost two CDs containing sensitive data pertaining to 25 million citizens. Additionally, when the facial recognition software was demonstrated to Baroness Anelay of St Johns, it failed twice. Why? The baroness was told her face was "too bland."

Terrorism will never be defeated in the traditional sense, only curtailed. The war on terror is not a temporary campaign, and any measures we introduce to fight it now will remain equally enduring. Governments may convince us of the need for increasing intrusion into our daily lives as part of the fight against terror, but when we give up our right to privacy, we are not only giving up our rights, but the rights of future generations. Citizens of the future might look back at the faith we put in today's governments and wonder how we could have been so naive.

The REAL ID Act in the U.S. Does Not Violate Privacy Rights

U.S. Department of Homeland Security

The U.S. Department of Homeland Security is responsible for protecting the United States against multiple threats, including ones to Web security, and for planning emergency response.

The 9/11 Commission recommended that the United States improve its ID system, and as a result, Congress passed the REAL ID Act of 2005. In a nationwide effort, the Department of Homeland Security has issued guidelines to improve state-issued driver's licenses in an attempt to fight terrorism and reduce fraud. Unfortunately, there are a number of myths surrounding REAL ID. REAL ID will not create a national ID card; states will continue to issue driver's licenses and identity cards. REAL ID will not create a national database, and it will not diminish individual privacy. Although departments of motor vehicles in various states may share information to verify a person's identity, the federal government will not be granted greater access. Finally, REAL ID is a funded mandate, supported by up to $150 million in grants in each year's federal budget.

R EAL ID is a nationwide effort to improve the integrity and security of state-issued driver's licenses and identification cards, which in turn will help fight terrorism and reduce fraud.

"Debunking the Myths," U.S. Department of Homeland Security, May 20, 2008. Reproduced by permission.

The 9/11 Commission recommended that the U.S. improve its system for issuing identification documents. In the Commission's words, "At many entry points to vulnerable facilities, including gates for boarding aircraft, sources of identification are the last opportunity to ensure that people are who they say they are and to check whether they are terrorists." The Commission specifically urged the federal government to "set standards for the issuance of sources of identification, such as driver's licenses." Congress responded to this key recommendation by passing the REAL ID Act of 2005. The Department of Homeland Security (DHS) was charged with implementing the regulations.

REAL ID defines the minimum standards necessary for identification cards being used for "official purposes" such as accessing federal facilities, boarding federally regulated commercial aircraft, and entering nuclear power plants. It also enhances the integrity and reliability of driver's licenses and identification cards, strengthens issuance capabilities, and increases security at driver's license and identification card production facilities.

MYTH: REAL ID creates a national identification (ID) card.

FACT: REAL ID simply sets minimum standards so that the public can have confidence in the security and integrity of driver's licenses and identification cards issued by all participating states and jurisdictions.

States and jurisdictions will maintain their ability to design and issue their own unique driver's licenses and identification cards. Each state and jurisdiction will continue to have flexibility with regard to the design and security features used on [each] card. Where REAL ID details the minimum data elements that must be included on the face of the card, most states and jurisdictions already include all or almost all of these data elements on their cards.

REAL ID identification documents will not be the only form of documentation accepted by the federal government or any other entity. You can still present another form of acceptable identification such as a U.S. passport, military ID, or government identification badge. If you do not have another form of acceptable documentation, however, you may experience delays at the airport due to the requirement for additional security screening.

MYTH: REAL ID creates a national database of personal information.

FACT: REAL ID requires that authorized DMV [Department of Motor Vehicles] officials have the capability to verify that an applicant holds only one valid REAL ID. REAL ID does not grant the federal government or law enforcement greater access to DMV data, nor does it create a national database.

States will continue to manage and operate databases for driver's license and identification card issuance.

REAL ID does not create a national database or require additional personal information on your driver's license than is already required by most states. It simply verifies the documents an applicant presents at the DMV to confirm the individual's identity and ensure that each individual has only one valid REAL ID.

DHS [Department of Homeland Security] recognizes the importance of protecting privacy and ensuring the security of the personal information.

Personally identifiable information, beyond the minimum information necessary to appropriately route verification queries, will not be stored.

MYTH: REAL ID will diminish privacy.

FACT: The REAL ID final rule calls on states to protect personal identity information. It requires each state to develop a security plan and lists a number of privacy and security elements that must be included in the plan.

The DHS Privacy Office has also issued *Best Practices for the Protection of Personally Identifiable Information Associated with State Implementation of the REAL ID Act,* which provides useful guidance to states on how to address the privacy and security of information related to REAL ID.

The REAL ID Act will not allow motor vehicle drivers' data to be made available in a manner that does not conform to the Driver's Privacy Protection Act. Furthermore, with REAL ID, DMV employees will be subject to background checks, a necessary step to protect against insider fraud, just one of the vulnerabilities to a secure licensing system. These steps raise the bar for state DMVs beyond what was previously required.

DHS recognizes the importance of protecting privacy and ensuring the security of the personal information associated with implementation of the REAL ID Act.

MYTH: DHS is creating a "hub" in order to gain access to Department of Motor Vehicle information.

FACT: An electronic verification hub will be designed to facilitate connectivity between the states and data owners to ensure that people applying for a REAL ID are who they say they are. The federal government will not gain greater access to DMV information as a result. Only authorized DMV officials and law enforcement will have access to DMV records.

REAL ID requires state DMVs to verify an applicant's identity document, date of birth, Social Security Number, residence and lawful status, as well as ensure that each individual has only one valid REAL ID. For example, the electronic verification hub will facilitate the state-to-state exchange of information to check for duplicate registrations in multiple states, therefore limiting the ability for persons to obtain multiple licenses for fraudulent purposes.

While DHS has pledged to fund the development and deployment of the hub, states will continue to manage and operate databases for driver's license and identification card issuance. DHS and the states will work together to ensure that security measures are in place to prevent unauthorized access or use of the information. Personally identifiable information, beyond the minimum information necessary to appropriately route verification queries, will not be stored.

MYTH: REAL ID is an unfunded mandate.

FACT: To date, approximately $90 million in dedicated grant funds have been offered by DHS to assist states with REAL ID implementation. This includes approximately $40 million in Fiscal Year (FY) 2006 and $50 million in FY 2008. An additional 20 percent of State Homeland Security Grant funds are discretionary and can be used for this purpose as well.

The President's Fiscal Year 2009 budget request includes up to $150 million in grants for states to implement REAL ID (up to $110 million from National Security and Terrorism Prevention Grants and, again, 20 percent of the State Homeland Security Grants).

DHS requested $50 million in Fiscal Year 2009 appropriated funds for the establishment of a state-owned and operated verification system. Furthermore, DHS cut the total costs to states by more than $10 billion, from an original estimate of $14.6 billion, to approximately $3.9 billion, a 73 percent reduction. States will continue to have discretionary authority to use up to 20 percent of their Homeland Security Grant funds for REAL ID implementation.

In order to focus the first phase of enrollment on those persons who may present the highest risk, DHS outlined an age-based enrollment approach to REAL ID allowing other individuals to be phased-in later. Phased-in enrollment eases the burden on states to re-enroll their entire driver's license and identification card population by providing additional time to accommodate the re-enrollment process.

8

Employee Privacy Rights Are Under Attack in the Workplace

Amy B. Crane

Amy B. Crane is an editor at Bankrate.

Although most Americans assume that they have the right of privacy, they may have very little privacy in the workplace. Today, employers have a number of methods to monitor employees' activities. This may include reviewing e-mails, video surveillance, drug testing, and monitoring Web surfing. Many employers worry that employees will waste time at inappropriate Web sites and possibly compromise company secrets. Employers may also monitor phone conversations and block access to unauthorized phone numbers; they frequently install video cameras in the workplace. While not legally required to do so, many employers inform employees that they are being monitored. Workers should be aware of this and avoid certain activities like personal e-mails while on the job.

Many Americans take their right to privacy for granted. But most don't realize that this right doesn't extend into the place where they spend most of their waking hours: their workplace.

"There is very little, if any, privacy in the workplace, particularly in the private sector," says Jeremy Gruber, legal director of the National Workrights Institute, an advocacy group

Amy B. Crane, "Workplace Privacy? Forget It!" Bankrate.com, July 18, 2005. Reproduced by permission.

for human rights in the workplace. "Privacy is one of the most-violated principles in the American workplace. People are aware to a degree how much monitoring goes on in the workplace, but most individuals are unaware of how pervasive the lack of privacy is."

Monitoring employees electronically and in other ways is a growing part of the way American companies do business, according to the 2005 Electronic Monitoring and Surveillance Survey, conducted by the American Management Association and the ePolicy Institute. According to the survey, which was released in May 2005, 76 percent of employers monitor workers' Web connections, while 50 percent store and monitor employees' computer files.

Types of Monitoring in the Workplace

Other types of monitoring at work can include:

- keyboard keystroke monitoring

- reviewing and storing employee e-mails and instant messages

- monitoring time spent on the phone, numbers called and actual taping of conversations

- video surveillance

- drug testing

- satellite technology to monitor use of company cars, cell phones and pagers

"There are three main reasons employers monitor employees: legal liability issues, employee productivity and security breaches," says Nancy Flynn, executive director of the ePolicy Institute. "For example, e-mail creates a written business record, and employers are becoming increasingly aware that e-mail and Internet activity is the electronic equivalent of DNA evidence. If a company is sued or investigated by a regu-

49

latory agency, you can take it to the bank that e-mail will be investigated and subpoenaed."

Computer-Related Monitoring

Employers are most concerned about employee use of company computers. This includes e-mail, instant messaging, Web surfing and files stored on company computers. According to the Electronic Monitoring Survey, 26 percent of employers who participated in the survey have fired workers for workplace offenses related to the Internet, while 25 percent of employers have fired employees for misuse of e-mail. While many employers monitor employees' Web surfing, a slightly smaller number—65 percent of those surveyed—actually use software to block workers' access to inappropriate Web sites.

Many employers are concerned about their employees' connecting to inappropriate Web sites, such as those with pornographic content or that allow employees to gamble online, Flynn says. Productivity suffers when employees spend too much time online surfing, attending to personal business or e-mailing friends. Employers also worry about workers' disclosing trade secrets or proprietary information over the Internet.

According to a 2004 ePolicy survey, instant messaging is one of the least-monitored computer activities—only 6 percent of employers surveyed at that time retained or archived instant messages, while 58 percent of employees surveyed use instant messaging for personal online conversations. "Most instant messaging takes place via free software tools that employees download and thus is outside employer firewalls," says Flynn. "We tell employers that if your employees are doing this, you are handing information over to outsiders."

Keyboard keystroke monitoring can track key words typed on a keyboard and can also track how fast employees are typing. "There is a problem with worker monitoring when it leads to an oppressive work environment," says Jay Stanley, communications director for the American Civil Liberties Union [ACLU] Technology and Liberty Project. "That can happen when employers can monitor things like keystrokes."

Video surveillance cameras may be installed in many areas of the workplace, including locker rooms, leading to a lack of privacy.

In such a situation, Stanley notes, employees can feel subtle or overt pressure to speed up the pace of their work, leading to morale problems.

Phone and Video Surveillance

Phone surveillance includes:

- monitoring and taping employee phone conversations

- blocking certain numbers such as 900 numbers

- monitoring time spent on the phone

- tracking numbers dialed

- taping and reviewing voice mail

- monitoring conversations between workers

According to the 2005 surveillance survey, 57 percent of employers surveyed block unauthorized phone numbers, and 51 percent monitor the amount of time spent on the phone and the numbers dialed. More than 80 percent of the employers who monitor these activities notify employees about what they are doing.

Employers use video surveillance in an effort to prevent theft, violence and sabotage, Flynn says. The survey states that 51 percent of employers surveyed use video monitoring. Of those, 85 percent notify workers of the practice. Video surveillance cameras may be installed in many areas of the workplace, including locker rooms, leading to a lack of privacy.

Besides computer, phone and video monitoring, new and older technologies give employees a wide variety of options to keep tabs on their employees. These other types of surveillance include:

Satellite technology. Satellite technology is rapidly evolving, and employers now have the ability to track employees through assisted global positioning or global positioning systems satellite using company cars, cell phones, pagers and smart cards. However, few of the employers surveyed are actually using these technologies—only 8 percent are tracking company cars, 5 percent track company cell phones and 8 percent track employee ID/smart cards.

Gruber notes that GPS gives employers the ability to track workers both on and off the job, and he recommends that employees use their own cell phones, handheld devices, computers and pagers while not working if they don't want to be monitored.

Drug testing. Some employers randomly test employees for drug use. Such tests can be the ultimate invasion of privacy as an employer may require an employee to provide a urine sample with a witness present, according to Gruber, who also notes that the courts have supported drug testing of private-sector employees in virtually all cases. "The problem with drug testing is that it doesn't determine whether a person is actually intoxicated on the job," he says. "It only indicates whether someone has been intoxicated in the past." In addition, these tests have an error rate and do give a certain percentage of false positives, leaving workers who don't do drugs at risk for discipline or termination even though they haven't done anything wrong. Gruber believes that employers should train supervisors to be aware of the signs of intoxication or drug use and provide employee assistance programs to help workers with addictions recover.

Flynn believes most employers are upfront about monitoring and that those with the best policies will tell employees what to expect in terms of monitoring. According to the 2005 Electronic Monitoring Survey, 80 percent to 89 percent of employers surveyed are notifying employees regarding computer-related monitoring.

Employee Notification

Beth Givens, executive director of the Privacy Rights Clearinghouse, urges employees to pay attention to their employers' policies. "Employers should notify employees that they are being monitored, what type of monitoring is being done, and how data from monitoring will be used," she says. "Also, workers should know what recourse they do have if the employer takes a negative or adverse action against them as a result of information obtained during monitoring."

> *Despite the fact that many employers notify employees about monitoring, the law doesn't require it.*

Flynn agrees that policies should be very specific and that employers should tell employees what is permissible in terms of personal use of e-mail, the Internet and company phones. "Your policy could say that employees are allowed to do these things for, say, 30 minutes a day or during lunch and on breaks," she says.

"A lot of companies will say that a limited amount of appropriate personal e-mail is allowed, but a limited amount is subject to interpretation. It might mean 15 minutes to one person and a few hours to someone else," she says. The ePolicy Institute also believes that monitoring should apply to all employees, including top executives.

Despite the fact that many employers notify employees about monitoring, the law doesn't require it, and many employers aren't specific about the type of monitoring done, Gruber says. Employers can also expand their monitoring programs without notifying employees and may just insert a blanket statement in their policy manual telling employees that they reserve the right to monitor, but not what types of monitoring are conducted.

What You Can Do About Workplace Privacy

Givens advises workers to be careful in their workplace activities to avoid problems with monitoring devices and programs. "Don't engage in activities that are contrary to your company's policies," she says. "This may include surfing the Web for non-work-related reasons. Be careful about who you share company information with online and over the phone."

With the workday stretching into employees' private lives and time, employers should be flexible about giving employees time for some personal communications at work, she says. "If you need to make a doctor's appointment or talk to your child's teacher, those activities may need to take place during the workday," she adds.

Gruber is concerned that even if employers are flexible about personal communications and activities at work, many of these communications are monitored, breaching employee privacy. "Monitoring is so pervasive that it rarely differentiates between business and personal information, so quite a bit of personal information can be determined about employees through monitoring," he says. "Even though technology exists that allows employers to be more specific in their monitoring to exclude personal information, they ignore it."

The ACLU's Stanley agrees.

"Many companies are hungry for more data and more information about their employees," he says. "But employers may need to re-examine the extent to which it is necessary to monitor their employees. This reflexive jump to adopt new technologies can give employers a feeling of control, but that can be illusory, especially if it denigrates the morale and trust in the workplace."

While private-sector employees have virtually no privacy rights, government employees do have established privacy rights and many union employees have more rights, not explicitly to privacy but to contest grounds for discipline or termination, Gruber says. He notes that virtually all private-sector employees can be terminated at will, for any or all reasons.

9

Ten Ways to Maintain Your Privacy at Work

Kate Lorenz

Kate Lorenz is the article and advice editor for CareerBuilder .com.

More than ever, companies are monitoring the behavior of their employees. This monitoring includes reviewing e-mail messages and using surveillance cameras. Organizations like Workplace Fairness believe that these practices violate a worker's privacy and have supported legislation to ensure workers' rights. In the meantime, employees need to follow a number of rules to avoid potential problems at work. First, they should be aware of company policy and avoid activities such as sending personal e-mail from work. Employees should keep passwords private and turn off computers when away from them. Workers should also avoid sensitive Web sites, keep personal information private (paycheck, paying bills), and never use a company credit card for personal purchases. Following these rules will help avoid potential conflicts around issues of privacy in the workplace.

From monitoring keystrokes to video surveillance to GPS satellite tracking, today's employers are keeping tabs on their employees.

According to a 2005 survey by the American Management Association (AMA), U.S. firms continue to record and review employee communications and activities on the job. This in-

Kate Lorenz, "10 Ways to Maintain Your Privacy at Work," CareerBuilder.com, September 24, 2009. Reproduced by permission.

cludes checking employee phone calls, e-mail messages, Internet connections and computer files.

Most observation takes place because of increased technology available to employees, such as e-mail and advanced online capabilities. Seventy-six percent of businesses monitor employee Web use, and 55 percent keep and review e-mail messages.

But companies are not just watching employees online. More than 51 percent of companies said they participate in video surveillance for security purposes. Thirty-one percent monitor employees' outgoing phone numbers. And if you use a key card to access your job, you work for one of the 53 percent of companies that use them.

Some groups think these practices violate employees' privacy rights. Organizations such as Workplace Fairness and the Privacy Rights Clearinghouse are working to bring about legislation that protects employees' rights to privacy in the workplace. Many companies, however, feel that since the equipment is company owned and operated, employees must adhere to company policies regarding personal use of technology.

Of the companies that watch employee behavior, 80 percent notify employees of this activity. Employers have established policies monitoring personal e-mail abuse (81 percent); personal instant messenger use (42 percent); operation of personal Web sites on company time (34 percent); personal postings on corporate blogs (23 percent); and operation of personal blogs on company time (20 percent).

And companies are increasingly putting their policies into action: 26 percent have fired workers for misusing the Internet, and another 25 percent have terminated employees for e-mail misuse.

So if privacy—and keeping your job—concern you, follow these tips for work:

1. Review your company's handbook.

Every company has a list of policies available to its employees. When you get a new job, your human resource department should make you aware of them. If you don't remember them, now's a good time to brush up on what's acceptable and not on the job.

2. Don't use company e-mail for private messages.

Although it may be tempting to forward the latest joke or urban legend to your colleagues, resist the urge. Someone in your organization—usually the network administrator—is watching all of the e-mails that come and go. Is this fair? According to experts, if your e-mail system is owned by your employer, the company is allowed to review its contents.

3. Always assume your messages will be shared with others.

It's all too easy for the recipient to hit "forward" rather than "reply" and send your message on to others. If the contents of your e-mail messages are meant to be private, pick up the phone and call the recipient instead of using e-mail.

4. Keep your passwords private.

If you don't want others to have access to your computer while you're out of the office, don't share your passwords. Keep them in a secure place where only you can find them.

5. Stay off sensitive Web sites while at work.

Although you may think you are cruising the 'Net inconspicuously, every time you visit a site you leave an electronic fingerprint. Your computer screen may also be in plain view of others who walk by your workspace. Visiting credit management sites, managing your bank account online, or shopping for lingerie could have the whole office talking about what you're viewing on your monitor.

6. Turn off your computer.

When you step away from your desk, turn off your computer. Anyone can click on your navigation bar to view the Web sites you've visited recently. Or worse, if you leave your e-mail open, a passerby could read your mail or even send a message under your account.

7. Pay your bills at home.

If you don't want your co-workers to know how much you owe on your credit cards or the size of your mortgage, keep your bills at home. These are private documents that your co-workers and employer do not need to see and that don't need to go through the corporate mailroom.

8. Keep your paycheck away from wandering eyes.

Put your paycheck in your pocket or purse as soon as you get it. Given the popularity of direct deposit these days, most people don't give payday a second thought. That can be a problem when paychecks are left lying around. Consider Kathy, an account manager at a national travel company. She recently moved to another cubicle and the co-worker who now occupied her empty desk found one of her old paychecks, opened it and shared the amount with others in the office.

9. Report to work on time.

According to one office administration manager in Chicago, "If your company has a security key card system that you use to gain access to your building, management knows what time you came into the building and reported for work. When needed, they can use these reports to implicate tardy employees." Surveillance cameras can also track employees' whereabouts and the time of their arrival and departure.

10. Don't use a company-issued credit card for personal purchases.

Many sales reps and executives receive corporate credit cards for business-incurred expenses. If you don't want the accounting department to know what size undies you wear, don't shop for clothing and other personal items with the company card.

If you are concerned about privacy and monitoring practices at your company, re-read your company handbook manual or ask your human resources department. Most businesses alert employees to the possibility that e-mail messages or online activities may be tracked. Keep in mind that your purpose at work is to—well—work, and realize that it's better to be safe than sorry. If you keep your personal e-mails to a minimum or avoid them altogether, make as few personal phone calls as possible and stay off the Internet, privacy shouldn't be an issue for you.

10

No Child Left Behind Violates High School Students' Privacy Rights

Kate Dittmeier Holm

Kate Dittmeier Holm is the author of "No Child Left Behind and Military Recruitment in High Schools."

Because of a provision within the No Child Left Behind Act (NCLB), schools are required to provide military recruiters with the personal contact information of students. Schools that fail to provide information may lose federal funding and/or be penalized in other ways. Schools must also provide access for military recruiters. Although parents can have their children removed from the information list, military recruiters still have access to students on school grounds. This access interferes with family privacy, and may—if challenged in court—prove unconstitutional. This access takes on special significance at a time when the United States is actively involved in conflicts in Iraq and Afghanistan. Because of this, it is important for parents, teachers, and school advisers to be aware of the potential influence of military recruiters. Schools should also make sure to inform parents of their option to opt out of the NCLB provision at the beginning of the school year.

I. Introduction

Military recruiters today have extensive access to high school students and their personal information. The No Child Left Behind Act (NCLB) and the National Defense Authorization

Kate Dittmeier Holm, "No Child Left Behind and Military Recruitment in High Schools: When Privacy Rights Trump a Legitimate Government Interest," *Journal of Law and Education*, vol. 36, October 2007, pp. 581–588. Reproduced by permission.

Act for Fiscal Year 2002 mandate that local educational agencies allow military recruiters access to secondary students' personal contact information. Schools must also provide recruiters the same access to students that post-secondary educational institutions and potential employers are afforded. Schools that violate these provisions risk the loss of federal funding along with intervention by the Department of Defense, the local educational agencies' elected representatives, and certain Congressional committees.

While parents may request in writing that their children's information not be disclosed to recruiters, schools must disclose students' information until such a request is made. Moreover, because recruiters are given the same access to students as are post-secondary educational institutions and other prospective employers, parents lack control over their children's exposure to recruiters. These mandates are troubling because they constitute a governmental intrusion into families' fundamental rights to privacy, or familial autonomy, which encompasses parents' rights to care for, rear, and control their children as they choose.

Exposure to military recruiters may conflict with a family's moral, religious, or other objection to military service. This additional exposure to military recruiters and aggressive recruiting tactics can influence the career paths of impressionable young adults. Without parents' knowledge of this exposure and influence, they may be deprived of an opportunity to start a meaningful dialogue at home about the pros and cons of military service.

Military recruitment in schools is of critical importance today given the U.S.'s active military operations in Iraq and Afghanistan, the high death toll as a result of those operations, troop shortages, military recruiting difficulties, and tenuous relations with North Korea and Iran. In light of these tumultuous current events, the right of privacy is essential so that parents can help their children make appropriate decisions about their futures, free from governmental intrusion.

Parents must also be able to protect their children from overly-aggressive recruiting tactics and wrongdoing by recruiters. The Government Accountability Office conducted a study in response to reports of recruiters' overly-aggressive tactics. The study found that during fiscal year 2004–2005, alleged incidents and armed services-identified incidents of recruiter wrongdoing increased from 4,400 cases to 6,600. During this period, criminal violations doubled. Further, the GAO found that the armed services lacked adequate oversight of recruiters to know the full extent of these violations and to prevent irregularities. Therefore, it is imperative that parents know recruiters have access to their children and that their consent is presumed.

Unless and until the courts strike down or Congress amends this provision, teachers and administrators must ensure students and their families know recruiters have access to their information and that they can opt out of sharing it, if they choose. Teachers and administrators, who are also influential in students' career paths after high school, need to be aware of the reach of recruiters and work with parents to ensure students make thoughtful and well-informed decisions. This may be achieved by providing information and encouragement regarding other choices that may be better suited for a student considering military service or impartially discussing the possibility of military service.

II. Overview of the Policy

Under NCLB and the National Defense Authorization Act, recruiters have access to secondary students' names, addresses, and telephone numbers unless parents request otherwise. Schools must inform parents of this only once and through "any method that is reasonably calculated" to inform them that recruiters will have access to their children's names, addresses, and phone numbers. This one-time-only notification must explain how to deny consent and the deadline for doing so.

Schools must also provide the same access to recruiters it provides to post-secondary educational institutions and other prospective employers. Schools often host functions, such as career or college fairs, in which recruiters from schools and employers visit to talk with students about their organizations and distribute information. Schools also often allow these types of representatives to visit during the school day. Regardless of an individual school's policies regarding how educational and non-military employment recruiters are given access to students, military recruiters are entitled to the same access under the NCLB Act. For this provision, the NCLB Act does not provide for parents to be able to opt out. Therefore, even if parents can choose not to expose their children to visits or phone calls from military recruiters by choosing not to release that information, they have no control over whether recruiters talk with their children at school or school functions where college or job recruiters are present.

Additionally, since recruiters are entitled to the "same access," if parents deny consent to release their children's names, addresses, or phone numbers to outside sources so as to avoid military recruiters, the result is that the school may not release them to post-secondary educational institutions and other prospective employers either. Therefore, when parents act to protect their children from the influence of military recruiters, a consequence is that students may not receive information from other desired sources, such as colleges, through their schools' release of their information to those sources.

Schools that violate the NCLB and National Defense Authorization Acts risk losing federal funding. Additionally, under the National Defense Act, officials from the Department of Defense, the local educational agencies' Congressional representatives, their Senators, their governor, and certain Congressional committees are notified to intervene in cases of non-compliance. The pressure that would be placed on a noncompliant local educational agency and the consequences of noncompliance would be enormous. Not only would a local educational agency suffer from a lack of federal funding, its elected officials would likely anticipate political repercussions over a loss of federal funding and pressure the agency to comply. Therefore, it would be virtually impossible for local educational agencies to refuse compliance. Indeed, the evidence shows that most schools do comply. The Department of Education reported in late 2002 that 95 percent of all secondary schools allowed a legally-compliant "degree of access" to military recruiters.

III. The Right to Family Privacy and Its Protections

This military recruitment policy in schools strikes at the heart of the constitutional right to privacy and the fundamental due process interests of parents in controlling their children, rearing their children, and determining who has access to their children. The United States Supreme Court has recognized the right to privacy in certain zones, including many situations relating to family autonomy and decision-making. One area in which the Court has long held that parents have a Fourteenth Amendment right to privacy is decision-making about their children's upbringing and education. In a case decided in 2000, the Court held that parents have a fundamental right to make decisions regarding the care, custody, and control of their children, including who, outside the nuclear family, may have access to their children. This is because fit parents are presumed to have their children's best interests in mind.

Fundamental rights are protected against governmental action, regardless of whether the procedures used to implement the action or policy are fair. Therefore, a law that implicitly or explicitly infringes on a fundamental Constitutional right is presumptively unconstitutional. To determine whether there is an infringement on a right, the Court considers the "directness and substantiality of the interference." If an infringement on a fundamental right is found, it requires strict scrutiny of the government's infringement on that right. For the government's infringement to be upheld, it must support a compelling government interest and be narrowly tailored to "effectuate only those interests," allowing the goveminent only "limited leeway" to do so. Moreover, the means selected by the government to achieve its objective cannot impinge on the right in question.

IV. The Laws' Effect on the Policy

The law at issue here presumes parental consent for military recruiters to access secondary school children to persuade them to engage in military service after high school. Parents may revoke their consent for information to be released, but consent is assumed until it is revoked. This is problematic because schools may inform parents of their right to opt out through "any means that is reasonably calculated" to inform them, including burying this information in a student handbook or handing out a notice at the beginning of a student's freshman year of high school with a myriad of other forms. Therefore, parents may not know that military recruiters have access to their children's information and that their consent has been assumed. Additionally, students may come in contact with recruiters at school or during career and college fairs, and parents have no way of denying consent for this. Essentially, this policy wrests control away from parents, thus implicating their fundamental rights to familial autonomy.

Next, the directness and substantiality of the interference with this right must be evaluated to determine whether there is an infringement. The government's representatives obtain students' information and contact them in order to persuade them to engage in military service after high school. They may also meet with students at events to which other types of recruiters have access. Parents are not asked to give permission to recruiters to contact their children. Instead, in the case of student information, recruiters are entitled to access and influence students unless and until parents invoke their right to deny consent, and children of parents who are unaware of this provision may be contacted against their parents' wishes. Moreover, parents have no way of knowing about or choosing to deny consent for their children meeting recruiters at the functions to which they have access. Thus, parental control is diminished by this policy and constitutes a direct and substantial interference with that fundamental right because it assumes parental consent until it is revoked. Therefore, this policy in the law is presumptively unconstitutional.

Military recruitment is no doubt a compelling and legitimate governmental interest. The policy in question supports that interest; however, the means chosen by the government to effectuate military recruitment are not the least-restrictive possible. Military recruitment can be achieved in narrower ways that do not infringe on family autonomy. Instead of a presumption of parental consent, parents should have to provide consent if they want their students to receive information from and be contacted by military recruiters. Military recruiting and college and job recruiting should also be held separately so that parents will know who will be recruiting their children at an event. With these policies, parents would then have the opportunity to make the informed choice whether to allow their children to interact with military recruiters and to thoughtfully consider and discuss with their children the possibility of military service after high school. Such a procedure would comport with the fundamental right of parents who desire to raise their children with certain religious beliefs or other values without governmental interference to the contrary. As it stands, this NCLB Act provision violates parents' rights to familial autonomy.

V. Solutions to Protect Students and Familial Autonomy

There are proactive steps concerned administrators and teachers can take, above and beyond the requirements of the law, to counteract the negative effects of this mandate unless and until Congress or the courts determine this practice is unconstitutional. Since parents must preemptively opt out of the release of their children's personal information to recruiters, high school administrators should inform students and parents of this requirement and make the appropriate forms available at the beginning of each school year. In doing so, parents can make choices for their families consistent with their beliefs and values and help their children plan for the future without recruiters' undue influence. Those forms should continue to be readily available throughout the school year for students and parents who may later decide to opt out.

Administrators, guidance counselors, and faculty must also work with parents to balance the increased influence of military recruiters to ensure students make an appropriate and informed career path decision, which may or may not include military service. Students should be provided with information and mentoring regarding college, technical college, and community college, as well as alternatives to military service for funding their educations. Students should also be counseled about the drawbacks of military service and about the profound choice they are making, especially given the allure of college scholarships, signing bonuses, and promises of adventure offered by recruiters.

VI. Conclusion

The military recruiter access policy of the NCLB Act and the National Defense Authorization Act of 2002 provides broad access to high school students for military recruiters. This policy is problematic because it infringes on a fundamental right of parents to rear their children in the way they see fit and to control who has access to their children. The current opt-out policy violates this right because it wrests control away from parents and assumes consent until it is revoked. Unless and until the Court recognizes that this violates parents' fundamental rights, teachers, guidance counselors, and administrators can take steps to ensure parents are informed about this policy and that students have information about a wide range of possibilities for the future so that each student makes appropriate choices, free from governmental intrusion.

11

No Child Left Behind Does Not Violate High School Students' Privacy Rights

Jody Feder

Jody Feder is a legislative attorney for the American Law Division.

The No Child Left Behind Act (NCLBA) carried a provision that allowed military recruiters access to students' personal information. The federal government ties compliance with the provision to federal funding: If schools do not cooperate, funding may be withheld. This provision has been controversial, however. Generally, the personal information includes names, phone numbers, and addresses. Although the opt-out procedure varies greatly from one school district to another, the NCLBA provision also allows parents to remove their children from the list. Recruiters are also allowed access to students on school grounds, though as with the opt-out procedure, schools have implemented this policy in a number of ways. While many believe that these policies deprive students of privacy, it seems unlikely that the courts would support this argument.

When Congress enacted the No Child Left Behind Act (NCLBA) of 2001, it added several new requirements regarding the ability of military recruiters to access student information and to approach students directly. These new provisions—which are different from similar Department of De-

Jody Feder, "Military Recruitment Provisions Under the No Child Left Behind Act: A Legal Analysis," CRS Report for Congress, January 8, 2008.

fense (DOD) provisions that allow DOD to compile directory information on high school students for military recruitment purposes or that require colleges and universities that receive federal funds to allow military recruiters on campus—have proven to be somewhat controversial. Proponents of the recruitment provisions argue that the new law allows recruiters to inform students about the military opportunities available to them and eases the task of recruiting volunteers to sustain the nation's military forces. On the other hand, opponents contend that the provisions raise concerns about student privacy and should be changed to make it easier to opt out. Currently, 95% of the country's school districts are estimated to be complying with the new requirements, although it is important to note that, traditionally, most schools had already allowed military recruiters to contact students long before the NCLBA provisions became mandatory.

Schools appear to have interpreted these opt-out provisions in a variety of ways.

The new NCLBA military recruitment provisions require high schools that receive federal funds to meet two requirements. First, such schools must "provide, on a request made by military recruiters . . . , access to secondary school students' names, addresses, and telephone listings," and second, schools must "provide military recruiters the same access to secondary school students as is provided generally to post secondary educational institutions or to prospective employers of those students." Schools that fail to comply with either of these two requirements—access to student information or equal access to students themselves—risk losing federal funds. However, private secondary schools that maintain a religious objection to military service are exempt from the recruitment provisions.

Access to Student Information

As noted above, schools must, when requested, provide military recruiters with information concerning student names, addresses, and telephone numbers. Unlike more personal information such as Social Security numbers, this type of data is not protected by the Family Educational Rights and Privacy Act (FERPA), which currently allows the release of student directory information in the absence of parental objections. Thus, even before the NCLBA provisions were enacted, such student contact information was potentially available to outside entities.

Like FERPA, the NCLBA also provides the opportunity to opt out of the provisions requiring the release of directory information to military recruiters. Under the NCLBA, students or their parents may request that the student's directory information not be released without prior written consent. In addition, the local educational agency or private school must notify parents of their right to make such a request.

Schools appear to have interpreted these opt-out provisions in a variety of ways. For example, some schools have, as part of their compliance with an array of privacy laws, issued a general notice informing parents that they can opt out of the release of student contact information, while other schools have issued a separate and more explicit notice informing parents that such information may be released to the military for recruitment purposes if the parents do not opt out. Both of these types of notice appear to meet the statutory requirement regarding informing parents of their right to opt out, but recipients of the latter type of notice may be more likely to exercise that option. As a result, the type of notice that a school elects to provide has been a subject of debate.

In addition, the notification provision has become controversial in part because schools have interpreted parental responses in different ways. For example, if parents fail to respond to the notice informing them of their right to opt out of the release of student information, some schools interpret the lack of response as indicating that the parent does not wish to opt out, while other schools interpret a lack of response as signifying that the parent does want to opt out. As a result, some interest groups have pressed legislators to clarify the law with regard to this point.

Equal Access to Students

In addition to requiring schools to provide access to student information, the NCLBA also requires schools to provide access to students themselves. Specifically, schools must provide military recruiters the same access to students as is otherwise provided to other recruiters, such as private employers or institutions of higher education. As with the notification provisions, schools have implemented the equal access provisions in a variety of ways. For example, some schools allow extensive access, permitting recruiters to set up information tables, visit classrooms, and freely approach students anywhere on campus. Other schools permit a lesser degree of access, and some restrict military access even further by forbidding information tables, requiring appointments before recruiters can meet students, and otherwise limiting access to campus. Despite these variations in school policy, schools are allowed to place as many or as few restrictions as they wish on military recruiters, as long as schools treat such recruiters the same way they treat other entities that wish to contact students.

Legal Concerns

As noted previously, some opponents of the NCLBA military recruitment provisions have raised legal concerns about the new requirements. In particular, some critics have questioned whether the recruitment provisions violate a student's right to privacy, but neither statutory nor constitutional analysis appears to support this argument. Indeed, from a statutory perspective, the NCLBA provisions regarding release of student contact information are, as noted above, entirely consistent with FERPA, the longstanding law that protects the educational privacy rights of students. Likewise, the NCLBA military recruitment provisions, for the reasons discussed below, do not appear to raise constitutional concerns.

Under the auspices of the Fourteenth Amendment, the Supreme Court has recognized that there is a constitutional right to privacy that protects against certain governmental disclosures of personal information, but it has not established the standard for measuring such a violation. In the absence of explicit standards, the circuit courts have tended to establish a series of balancing tests that weigh the competing privacy interests and government interests in order to determine when information privacy violations occur.

In *Falvo ex rel. Pletan v. Owasso Independent School District No. I-011*, the Court of Appeals for the Tenth Circuit weighed the plaintiff's claim that peer grading and the practice of calling out grades in class resulted in an impermissible release of her child's education records in violation of FERPA. The plaintiff also claimed that the practice of peer grading violated her child's constitutional right to privacy. Although the court, in a holding that was later reversed by the Supreme Court, ruled that the practice of peer grading violated FERPA, the Tenth Circuit denied the plaintiff's constitutional claim. In rejecting this claim, the court applied a three-part balancing test that considers "(1) if the party asserting the right has a legitimate expectation of privacy, (2) if disclosure serves a compelling state interest, and (3) if disclosure can be made in the least intrusive manner." Based on the first prong of this test, the Tenth Circuit rejected the plaintiff's constitutional claim because it ruled that students' school work and test grades were not highly personal matters that deserved constitutional protection.

Like peer-graded student homework assignments, the release of student names, addresses, and telephone numbers to military recruiters would probably not be viewed by a court as violating a student's constitutional right to privacy under such a balancing test. Unlike Social Security numbers or medical records, for example, it is unlikely that a court would hold that individuals have a legitimate expectation of privacy in the type of basic contact information that is typically found in a phone book. Furthermore, the government could argue persuasively that the release of such information serves a compelling state interest in facilitating the maintenance of the nation's armed forces. Finally, a court would probably view the disclosure required by the NCLBA as minimally intrusive, given that students can either opt out of the information release or decline to join the military, or both.

Ultimately, a court reviewing any privacy-based challenge to the NCLBA military recruitment provisions would be likely to reject such a claim, especially in light of the fact that Congress was clearly acting within the scope of its constitutional authority when it enacted the military recruitment provisions of the NCLBA. Under the Spending Clause of the Constitution, Congress frequently promotes its policy goals by conditioning the receipt of federal funds on state compliance with certain requirements. Indeed, the Supreme Court "has repeatedly upheld against constitutional challenge the use of this technique to induce governments and private parties to cooperate voluntarily with federal policy," and the Court recently reaffirmed this principle when, in response to a First Amendment challenge, it upheld similar military recruitment provisions that apply to colleges that receive federal funds. Thus, the Court would likely uphold the NCLBA provisions in part on the basis of congressional authority under the Spending Clause.

12

A National Medical Records Database May Threaten Privacy Rights

Bernadine Healy

Bernadine Healy is the health editor for U.S. News & World Report.

Patients expect doctors to honor privacy, respecting the oath they have taken. But many patients wonder whether this assumed right of privacy will be maintained if medical records are placed on a national database. A national electronic database, in fact, is one of the first priorities of health care reform. Without strict privacy, though, many patients may be less forthcoming with information: If the information is accidentally released, it cannot be taken back. The Institute of Medicine (IOM) believes that there are many advantages to a national database of medical records, but the organization also believes that the U.S. government's current standard for privacy is inadequate. One IOM measure would allow a patient to know who has reviewed her medical records. Whatever measures the government takes in relation to this new health policy, it must ensure privacy to maintain the integrity of the database.

Doctors are supposed to be nosy. It's not just that they examine your naked body inside and out and record all its imperfections. Physicians are trained to peer into your life, past and present, and ask all sorts of sensitive, if not uncomfortable, questions. Have you ever used marijuana or cocaine? How about steroids? How many sexual partners? Ever had a sexually transmitted disease? An abortion? Had sex with the same sex? How much do you smoke or drink? Have you used Botox or had plastic surgery? Have you been depressed or been treated for mental illness? And how about your marriage—or marriages?

You get the gist; the experience is intrusive. But the doctor-patient relationship was never meant to be other than confidential and privileged and solely for the benefit of the patient. Patients expect it, or they would not be forthcoming. And doctors take the Hippocratic oath, pledging to hold sacred their patients' secrets. This pledge of confidentiality, however, is now challenged by a world where computers rule and health information falls into many hands. One might well ask whether medical privacy is just too outmoded a concept for today's information-hungry world.

We had better decide. Electronic medical records have become a national goal, a way to replace the highly fragmented and inefficient paper system used in most medical settings today. President Obama has made revamping the medical system a top priority, with the national electronic medical record first up in healthcare reform. Indeed, the economic stimulus package assigns billions of dollars to that effort. In light of public sensitivity, this major jump-start for centralized records comes with provisions to further strengthen privacy laws.

However much we Facebook or Twitter about personal stuff, the public remains jittery about losing control of personal health information. Americans treasure their zone of privacy, and polls show they fear that government does not protect nearly well enough the medical information it already accesses. Clearly, once sensitive information is out there, it can't be brought back.

Look at Alex Rodriguez. A breached pledge to keep confidential those urine tests for steroids taken in 2003 has left his career a shambles, and 103 other players are waiting for their results to be leaked to the press, too. Their past transgressions notwithstanding, more than 1,000 ballplayers consented to these tests back then, with the understanding that results would be anonymous. The findings were to be destroyed after the league assessed the magnitude of the problem. (In a similar design years ago, anonymous HIV testing studies helped reveal the size of the AIDS epidemic.) The players' data led to what are now stringent drug testing and penalties, as there were none at the time.

It's easy to translate this situation to a violated personal medical record or, on a larger scale, a research study. Imagine if researchers culled the national health record for information on sensitive groups, whether they be HIV carriers or illegal-drug users. If one of the subjects in the study were under government investigation, might not the other records be sucked up in a sting? Not too far-fetched.

The Institute of Medicine [IOM] issued a report on privacy of medical records in early February that fuels this concern. The IOM started with the premise that protections for electronic medical records are a must, because the benefit of health IT [information technology] is so great. The records will speed up access to a patient's health information, cut down on redundant care, and reduce medical errors. Access to the online digital record by researchers also means massive medical databases can be searched, shared, analyzed, and drawn upon. Epidemiological research would be carried out on a scale never before imagined, to improve care, develop better practice guidelines, and determine cost-effectiveness.

Recognizing the importance of the public's confidence in the sanctity and confidentiality of medical records, the IOM came down hard on the current privacy protections that are supposed to ensure this. The group concluded that government rules to protect patients' medical records are simply inadequate. At best, they should be scrapped—or overhauled, at the very least. The report also points to the many security breaches of medical record databases, covering tens of thousands of patients, that have occurred in the past two years, and cites this as a growing problem.

Lack of confidentiality protections for a far more extensive national online record system would surely cause major unrest among most Americans. Despite its shortcomings, the paper record distributed across hospitals and doctors' offices has a limited ability for wide dissemination. A centralized, integrated, electronic record with access to all Americans' files would not only contain more information, but its potential distribution could be measured in the millions, not just the few who could lay their hands on a chart. Would most of those unauthorized eyeballs be gazing for the patient's benefit? Don't think so.

One thing that the IOM calls for is an audit trail of just who accesses online records. In fact, there is no reason that patients themselves should not know who's seen their records, rightly or wrongly, here or elsewhere in the world, where records are now outsourced for insurance review. It's also unseemly that marketers can buy pharmacy information about patients, so they can send them illness-specific advertising, and questionable that insurance companies should send patients mailings that suggest they take a medicine other than the one their doctor has ordered.

Complacency on the part of government about going after violations of medical privacy has stirred up patient concerns. So has the lack of informed consent when researchers use patients' records for studies. Some have complained it's almost impossible to correct mistakes once an electronic record has been created. And if patients visit their doctors imagining that the medical information they provide, which is being typed and sent into a centralized national medical record system before their eyes, might be seen by their employer or just some busybody, they will no doubt be tempted to hide things.

The feds' clout and resources will make the national medical record happen. But to ensure that that record is an accurate and sturdy backbone of a more efficient, safe, and accountable health system, patient privacy is paramount. And now is the time to admit that protecting privacy has not been one of our nation's strong suits.

Cell Phones Have the Potential to Violate Privacy in School

Cara Branigan

Cara Branigan is an associate editor at eSchool Media.

Many observers fear that cell phones with cameras will invade other peoples' right of privacy. For instance, a student may take a camera phone into a locker room or use a camera phone to take pictures of a test. A number of schools have adopted policies that restrict the use of cell phones and camera phones in school. Nonetheless, there are millions of cell phones, and it is virtually impossible to oversee every phone. A number of public and private clubs have banned camera phones from the premises to protect both customers' and employees' privacy. Despite these concerns, it has been reported that camera phone abuse is seldom a problem in the United States. In many countries, however, camera phones have created a greater social disruption, leading to legal penalties.

Picture this scenario: A student is changing in his school's locker room when a teammate or classmate takes out a cell phone, ostensibly to call home for a ride. That night, a compromising photo of the student appears online—taken with his classmate's cell phone when the student least expected it.

Cara Branigan, "Camera Phones Call Up Privacy Fears For Schools," eSchool News, January 12, 2004. Reproduced by permission. Visit http://www.eschoolnews.com for daily news and resources for K-12 educators.

Thanks to the latest advances in cell phone technology, this scenario is now entirely possible—and that has some policy makers and school leaders concerned.

After the Columbine High School shootings in 1999 and the Sept. 11 terrorist attacks two years later, a number of school systems and state legislatures across the nation relaxed their rules on cell phone use by students on campus. Now, however, the emergence of camera cell phones has created a whole new set of privacy and data-protection issues for school officials to address.

"The potential for using those devices for negative uses is certainly there," said David Dahl, principal of Armstrong High School in Plymouth, Minn.

Cell Phone Misuse

Besides invading a student's privacy in a locker room, bathroom, or other private place, educators worry the inconspicuous look of camera-equipped cell phones could make it easier for students to cheat on something like a test. If a student takes a test and manages to photograph it with his cell phone, for example, it would take just seconds for the image to be distributed throughout the school.

Most schools already have rules in place that address the presence of traditional cell phones—but the increasing popularity of camera cell phones in the United States has led some forward-looking administrators to adopt policies governing the use of these devices as well.

"We've had a policy for 'nuisance' objects—no pagers, no CD players—so we've just incorporated cell phones and camera cell phones [into those rules]," Dahl said.

"I think we're ahead of any potential problems," said Steve Degenaar, principal of Apple Valley High School, also in Minnesota. Students at Apple Valley are still allowed to have camera-equipped phones at school—but like regular cell phones, they must not be seen or heard on school property.

But enforcing these policies could be a problem.

"Kids have always had cameras, but it's not something they always carry with them in school," Degenaar said. "Cell phones are personal property, and there are literally hundreds of them. It's much more difficult to control."

"Spy-Cams"

Technology market research firm International Data Corp. estimates there are about six million camera-equipped cell phones in the United States.

A number of health clubs, gyms, swimming pools, public bathrooms, and even strip clubs have banned the use of camera phones to safeguard customers and employees.

A recent television advertisement by Sprint Corp. hypes the "spy-cam" potential of these devices when a woman secretly snaps a picture of a sloppy eater in a cafeteria and sends it to her friend with the note, "Here's your new boyfriend."

Though many photos are deleted before they are printed, archived, or downloaded to a computer, others are uploaded to the internet.

Mobile web logs, also known as "moblogs," are gaining in popularity. One user on Buzznet.com, for example, showcased his experience at the recent MacWorld conference, complete with photos of Apple Computer's booth, the company's new iPod, and what seem like pictures of random people at the conference. On Fotolog.net, one user logs photos of homeless people.

Cell Phone Bans

No widespread instances of camera phone abuse have been reported yet in the United States, but a number of health clubs, gyms, swimming pools, public bathrooms, and even strip clubs have banned the use of camera phones to safeguard customers and employees.

The YMCA of Greater Louisville, Ky., banned the use of camera phones for staff and parents involved in its children's programs. "Our first concern was for some of our children's programs," Steve Tarver, president of the YMCA of Greater Louisville, told the city's *Courier-Journal.* "We've had no incidents or problems at this point, but we have a staff group studying camera-phone use in our total facility."

Des Peres, Mo., a suburb of St. Louis, created a penalty for using camera phones in places where people expect privacy. In Warwick, R.I., Councilwoman Sue Stenhouse proposed outlawing camera phones at city buildings with locker rooms. In December, the Chicago City Council banned the use of camera phones in public bathrooms, locker rooms, and showers.

Last November, Elk Grove, Ill., a Chicago suburb, banned all cell phones in public locker rooms, whether they could take photos or not. "There is no reason to have a cell phone while you're changing and showering," Elk Grove Commissioner Ron Nunes told the *New York Times.* "I'd rather protect the children and the public more than someone who wants to call home and see what's for dinner."

U.S. Rep. Michael G. Oxley, R-Ohio, and Sen. Mike DeWine, R-Ohio, also reportedly broadened the language of the federal Video Voyeurism Prevention Act of 2003 to prohibit the use of camera phones in restrooms in federal buildings.

"Our bill would only apply to federal property, but it would spur the states to pass similar legislation," Oxley told the *New York Times.*

An International Phenomenon

The Cellular Telecommunications and Internet Association asserts that camera phone abuse in the United States is rare.

In Japan, however, people have gone to jail for photographing up women's skirts. Also, some Japanese residents reportedly have started "digital shoplifting" in bookstores by photographing and eMailing pictures of copyrighted material.

In Scotland, police reportedly use camera phones to help track down graffiti vandals. Police snap pictures of scribbles and doodles on school books and then compare them to photos of the "tags," or signatures, that vandals use to mark their graffiti.

Police say this method has improved the success of their vandalism detective work by 18 percent, the *Scottish Daily Record* reported.

Another Scottish paper, Glasgow's *Evening Times*, reported that the Scottish Secondary Teachers' Association has called for a ban on camera phones to prevent cheating and to keep pictures of students from getting into the hands of pedophiles.

14

Cell Phone Privacy Should Be Respected at School

American Civil Liberties Union of Colorado

The American Civil Liberties Union of Colorado is a branch of the American Civil Liberties Union and is dedicated to the defense of First Amendment rights.

In May of 2007, at Monarch High School in Boulder, Colorado, school officials confiscated a number of cell phones from students in relation to a suspected infraction of school rules. After confiscating the cell phones, school officials transcribed students' text messages and placed the transcripts in the students' school files. The school's actions involved more than a dozen students and represented an abuse of authority. Repeatedly, school officials misled parents and students in regard to the confiscation of cell phones. While Monarch High School stated that students have no right of privacy while on school grounds, this is simply false. In fact, the actions of school officials violate a number of criminal statutes that carry heavy penalties.

To the members of the Boulder Valley School District [BVSD] Board of Education:

We write to ask you to resolve a serious civil liberties issue at Monarch High School. Monarch Administrators have been unjustifiably violating students' right of privacy by unreasonably confiscating their cell phones and reading and transcribing students' text messages. Administrators have reportedly

"Letter to Boulder Valley School District Board of Education," American Civil Liberties Union of Colorado, October 10, 2007. Reproduced by permission.

declared that a student has no right of privacy while in school, and they have reportedly claimed the right to read any and all text messages they please.

Monarch administrators could not be more wrong. Students *do* have rights of privacy, and those rights are protected not only by the state and federal constitutions, but also by Colorado statutes that carry serious criminal penalties. The actions of Monarch administrators have violated these Colorado criminal statutes and the constitutional rights of Monarch students.

We ask the Board of Education to take action. Administrators at Monarch High School must stop seizing and searching students' cell phones in violation of state and federal law.

The ACLU [American Civil Liberties Union] learned of the actions of Monarch administrators in multiple interviews with Monarch students and their parents. The interviews began with students' complaints about a series of interrogations that took place at the end of the 2006–2007 school year, during which their cell phones were seized and their text messages searched and transcribed. Follow-up conversations with the parents also included complaints that administrators were less than forthcoming and even disrespectful in the manner in which they handled parents' concerns about the investigation of their children. The following summarizes what the ACLU learned in these interviews:

Confiscating Cell Phones

On May 24th, 2007, the school's security officer detained a student who was accused of violating two school rules: one that prohibited him from being in a particular parking lot, and another that forbids smoking cigarettes. The investigation of these relatively minor violations of school rules soon led to a series of interrogations in which administrators questioned numerous students and carried out a wholesale search of multiple cell phones.

The security guard delivered the student to the office of Drew Adams, assistant principal of Monarch High School. Adams ordered the student to empty his pockets and his backpack, presumably to look for cigarettes. No cigarettes were found, nor did the search uncover evidence of any other infractions. At that point, the search should have ended. Monarch administrators, however, were determined to go much further.

Adams asked the student to turn over his cell phone. The student protested and asked Adams why he wanted the phone. Adams replied that the phone "was a distraction," and he did not want the student to send text messages while he was detained in the principal's office. After confirming that the cell phone was turned off, the student reluctantly surrendered it. Adams took the phone and left the office.

When Adams returned some time later, it became immediately clear that he had not been truthful about the reason he wanted the student's cell phone. Adams declared that he had read the phone's text messages and had found some that mentioned marijuana that he characterized as "incriminating."

Adams began interrogating the student about the text messages. The student asked that his mother be present, and Adams agreed to call her. When the student's mother arrived, she learned that Adams had not merely read the text messages—he had also transcribed many of them. He produced a copy of the transcribed messages, which administrators eventually placed in the student's disciplinary file. The disciplinary files of additional students soon contained transcripts of text messages found on their cell phones.

Interrogations and Cell Phone Searches

The student's mother wanted the cell phone returned, but Adams insisted on keeping it over the Memorial Day weekend. When the student's mother finally recovered it the following Tuesday, she discovered that Adams had apparently drafted a text message and had attempted to send it from her son's phone to one of her son's friends. The text message appeared in the phone's outbox with an unambiguous time and date stamp showing that it was drafted while Adams had possession of the phone. The text message itself appeared to be Adams' attempt to engage the receiving student in a conversation while Adams was falsely representing himself as a student.

Monarch High School authorities followed up with a cascade of additional interrogations accompanied by seizures and searches of additional students' cell phones. In conjunction with assistant principals Julie Wheeler [and] Mark Sibley and Principal Barbara Spelman, Adams used the names found in the first student's text messages to call in more students, interrogate them, seize their cell phones, scour through their personal text messages, and transcribe additional text messages that administrators deemed to be "incriminating." Using more names gathered in this second round of questioning, school administrators expanded the runaway investigation with yet another wave of interrogations and cell phone searches. In one case, Adams held one of the students' cell phones in his hand, and while the student was detained in the office, Adams read and transcribed incoming text messages as they arrived.

School administrators repeatedly misled students and parents in order to gain possession of the students' cell phones.

Abuse of Authority

The ACLU spoke with many of the parents and [more than] a dozen students who were drawn into these successive waves of interrogations and cell phone searches. The ACLU did not speak with everyone, so the total number of students affected is certainly higher. From these interviews, a number of patterns emerge.

First, it is clear that Monarch school administrators believe, erroneously, that they have an unfettered right to seize a student's cell phone and rummage through and transcribe any and all text messages they find. When students questioned whether Adams had the authority to read their text messages, he replied that when they were on school property, he had the right to read any text messages he wanted. Similarly, Principal Spelman reportedly told one parent that Monarch High School students simply had no privacy rights.

Second, school administrators repeatedly misled students and parents in order to gain possession of the students' cell phones. Most students report being told by school administrators that they wanted to take custody of the cell phone only to prevent text messaging during the meeting. Parents report receiving the same false assurances. In one case, a student who had initially balked at surrendering his cell phone did so on his mother's instruction after Mr. Adams called the mother and claimed that the only reason he needed it was to prevent any disrupting use of the phone during his meeting with the student.

Contrary to the statements of Monarch administrators, students do indeed have privacy rights while in school, and those rights are protected by law.

Third, school administrators hindered students' efforts to involve their parents and obstructed concerned parents' efforts to obtain accurate and complete information about the school's investigation of their children. Two students reported that over an extended period of time, they repeatedly requested and were denied an opportunity to call their parents. In one case, a student was denied permission to call his parents even though the school day had long since ended and his parents were expecting his call. Parents endured repeated delays and what they perceived as callous carelessness and bureaucratic evasiveness when they tried to obtain accurate and timely copies of the transcripts of their children's text messages, transcripts which administrators placed in students' permanent files. School officials delivered the transcript of one student's text messages to the parents of an entirely different student. Parents also complained about inaccurate transcripts. For example, a student who was merely the passive recipient of a transcribed text message was erroneously identified as the sender.

Finally, it appears that this is not the first time that Monarch High School administrators have abused their authority to seize and search students' text messages. While the wave of successive searches and interrogations conducted in May of 2007 is an especially egregious example, students and parents also mentioned two additional incidents in which Monarch school administrators seized students' cell phones and searched through their text messages. Indeed, parents report that the actions of Monarch administrators have been endorsed and ratified by the school district's legal counsel. Without action from the BVSD Board of Education, similar abuses are likely to occur in the future.

Violation of Criminal Statutes

The BVSD Board of Education must take action to educate Monarch High School administrators and put a stop to these abuses. Contrary to the statements of Monarch administrators, students do indeed have privacy rights while in school, and those rights are protected by law. The actions of Monarch High School authorities violate state and federal constitutional provisions that forbid unreasonable searches and seizures. They also violate Colorado statutes that carry serious criminal penalties. . . .

In conclusion, Monarch High School administrators have violated Colorado criminal statutes that are designed to protect the privacy of telephonic and electronic communications, as well as state and federal constitutional provisions that prohibit unreasonable searches and seizures. They have declared that Monarch students have no rights of privacy that administrators are bound to respect. Without intervention by the Boulder Valley School District Board of Education, there is every indication that Monarch administrators will continue this flagrant disregard for the rights of students and the rule of law. It is imperative that the Board of Education intervene forcefully. The Board must direct administrators to stop conducting these cell phone searches that violate state and federal law.

Organizations to Contact

The editors have compiled the following list of organizations concerned with the issues debated in this book. The descriptions are derived from materials provided by the organizations. All have publications or information available for interested readers. The list was compiled on the date of publication of the present volume; the information provided here may change. Readers need to remember that many organizations take several weeks or longer to respond to inquiries.

American Civil Liberties Union (ACLU)
125 Broad Street, 18th Floor, New York, NY   10004
(212) 549-2500 • fax: (212) 549-2646
e-mail: aclu@aclu.org
Web site: www.aclu.org

The ACLU is a national organization that defends Americans' civil rights as guaranteed in the U.S. Constitution. It advocates for freedom of all forms of speech, including pornography, flag burning, and political protest. The ACLU offers numerous reports, fact sheets, and policy statements on free speech issues, which are freely available on its Web site. Some of these publications include "Free Speech Under Fire," "Freedom of Expression," and, for students, "Ask Sybil Liberty About Your Right to Free Expression."

American Library Association (ALA)
50 E. Huron Street, Chicago, IL   60611
(800) 545-2433 • fax: (312) 440-9374
e-mail: ala@ala.org
Web site: www.ala.org

The ALA is the United States' primary professional organization for librarians. Through its Office for Intellectual Freedom (OIF), the ALA supports free access to libraries and library

materials. The OIF also monitors and opposes efforts to ban
books from libraries. Its publications, which are freely available on its Web site, include "Intellectual Freedom and Censorship Q & A," the "Library Bill of Rights," and the "Freedom
to Read Statement."

The Brookings Institution
1775 Massachusetts Ave. NW, Washington, DC   20036
(202) 797-6000 • fax: (202) 797-6004
e-mail: brookinfo@brook.edu
Web site: www.brookings.org

The institution, founded in 1927, is a think tank that conducts
research and education in foreign policy, economics, government, and the social sciences. In 2001, it began America's Response to Terrorism, a project that provides briefings and
analysis to the public and which is featured on the center's
Web site. Other publications include periodic *Policy Briefs* and
books such as *Terrorism and U.S. Foreign Policy.*

Cato Institute
1000 Massachusetts Ave. NW, Washington, DC   20001-5403
(202) 842-0200 • fax: (202) 842-3490
e-mail: cato@cato.org
Web site: www.cato.org

Cato is a nonpartisan public policy research foundation dedicated to limiting the role of government and protecting individual liberties. It publishes the quarterly magazine *Regulation*, the bimonthly *Cato Policy Report*, and numerous policy
papers and articles. "Understanding Privacy—and the Real
Threats to It" and "Why Canning 'Spam' Is a Bad Idea" are
among its works.

Electronic Frontier Foundation (EFF)
454 Shotwell Street, San Francisco, CA   94110-1914
(415) 436-9333 • fax: (415) 436-9993
e-mail: information@eff.org
Web site: www.eff.org

EFF is a nonprofit, nonpartisan organization that works to protect privacy, freedom of speech and other rights in the digital world. Fighting censorship on the Internet is one of its core missions. Its publications, which are freely available on its Web site, include a "Legal Guide for Bloggers" and white papers such as "Noncommercial Email Lists: Collateral Damage in the Fight Against Spam."

Federal Bureau of Investigation (FBI)
935 Pennsylvania Ave. NW, Room 7972
Washington, DC   20535-0001
(202) 324-3000
Web site: www.fbi.gov

The FBI, the principal investigative arm of the U.S. Department of Justice, investigates specific crimes assigned to it and provides other law enforcement agencies with cooperative services, such as fingerprint identification, laboratory examinations, and police training. The mission of the FBI is to uphold the law through the investigation of violations of federal criminal law and to protect the United States from foreign intelligence and terrorist activities in a manner that is faithful to the U.S. Constitution. Press releases, congressional statements, and major speeches are available on the agency's Web site.

Federal Trade Commission (FTC)
600 Pennsylvania Ave. NW, Washington, DC   20580
(877) FTC-HELP (382-4357)
Web site: http://www.ftc.gov/index.shtml

The FTC works to ensure that the nation's markets are vigorous, efficient, and free of restrictions that harm consumers. The FTC enforces federal consumer protection laws that prevent fraud, deception, and unfair business practices and it combats identity theft, Internet scams, and telemarketing fraud. Publications posted on the FTC Web site offer consumer information concerning telemarketing, credit cards, and identity theft.

Foundation for Individual Rights in Education (FIRE)
601 Walnut Street, Suite 510, Philadelphia, PA   19106
(215) 717-3473 • fax: (215) 717-3440
e-mail: fire@thefire.org
Web site: www.thefire.org

FIRE was founded in 1999 to defend the rights of students and professors at American colleges and universities. The group advocates for and provides legal assistance to students and professors who feel that their individual rights, particularly their rights to free speech, have been violated. Its publications include *FIRE's Guide to Free Speech on Campus* and "Spotlight: The Campus Freedom Resource," the latter of which contains information about speech codes at specific colleges and universities.

Health Privacy Project
1634 I Street NW, # 1000, Washington, DC   20006
(202) 637-9800 • fax: (202) 637-0968
e-mail: info@healthprivacy.org
Web site: www.cdt.org/issue/health-privacy

Founded in 1997, the Health Privacy Project is dedicated to raising public awareness of the importance of ensuring health privacy in order to improve health care access and quality, both on an individual and a community level. The project provides research studies, policy analyses, congressional testimony, and other information for anyone concerned with health care issues. It publishes fact sheets, editorials, press releases, privacy regulation guides, and reports on health privacy.

The Heritage Foundation
214 Massachusetts Ave. NE, Washington, DC   20002-4999
(202) 546-4400 • fax: (202) 544-2260
e-mail: pubs@heritage.org
Web site: www.heritage.org

The Heritage Foundation is a conservative public policy research institute that supports the principles of free enterprise and limited government in environmental matters. Its many publications include the monthly *Policy Review* and position papers concerning terrorism, privacy rights, and constitutional issues.

National Retail Federation (NRF)

325 Seventh Street NW, Suite 1100, Washington, DC 20004
(800) NRF-HOW2 (673-4692) • fax: (202) 737-2849
Web site: www.nrf.com

NRF is a retail trade association with membership that includes retail stores and distributors such as department, discount, catalog, and Internet stores. It aims to expand and improve the retail workforce. The federation opposes privacy legislation that it believes would place too many restrictions on marketers, would burden businesses with too many requirements, or would impede the growth of the Internet. NRF distributes the daily e-mail newsletter *NRF SmartBrief*, the *Weekly Tax Update*, and the monthly *Retail Trade Issues*.

National Security Agency (NSA)

9800 Savage Road, Fort Meade, MD 20755-6704
(301) 688-6524
Web site: www.nsa.gov

The NSA coordinates, directs, and performs activities that protect American information systems and produce foreign intelligence information. The NSA employs satellites to collect data from telephones and computers, aiding in the fight against terrorism. Speeches, briefings, and reports are available on its Web site.

National Workrights Institute

166 Wall Street, Princeton, NJ 08540
(609) 683-0313
e-mail: info@workrights.org
Web site: www.workrights.org

The National Workrights Institute was founded in January 2000 by the former staff of the American Civil Liberties Union's National Taskforce on Civil Liberties in the Workplace. The institute's goal is to improve the legal protection of human rights in the workplace and to see that employment laws are adequately enforced and strengthened. The institute publishes annual reports and provides information for articles in newspapers, national magazines, and television shows including *ABC World News Tonight*.

Office of the Privacy Commissioner of Canada
112 Kent Street, Place de Ville, Tower B, Third Floor
Ottawa, Ontario K1A 1H3
(613) 947-1698 • fax: (613) 947-6850
e-mail: publications@privcom.gc.ca
Web site: www.privcom.gc.ca

An advocate for the privacy rights of Canadians, the Privacy Commissioner of Canada investigates complaints from individuals with respect to the federal public sector and the private sector, conducts audits, and promotes awareness of privacy issues. The Privacy Commissioner's Web site details Canada's privacy legislation, provides privacy impact assessments, and offers various fact sheets. Its Resource Centre contains such publications as the office's annual reports to Parliament, official speeches, and privacy rights guides for businesses and individuals.

Privacy International, Washington Office
1718 Connecticut Ave. NW, Suite 200, Washington, DC 20009
(202) 483-1217 • fax: (202) 483-1248
e-mail: privacyint@privacy.org
Web site: www.privacy.org

Privacy International is an independent, nongovernmental organization whose goal is to protect the privacy rights of citizens worldwide. On its Web site, the organization provides archives of material on privacy, including international agreements, the report *Freedom of Information and Access to Government Records Around the World*, and *Private Parts Online*, an online newsletter that reports recent stories on international privacy issues.

Privacy Rights Clearinghouse (PRC)
3100 Fifth Ave., Suite B, San Diego, CA   92103
(619) 298-3396 • fax: (619) 298-5681
e-mail: jbeebe@privacyrights.org
Web site: www.privacyrights.org

The PRC is a nonprofit consumer organization with a two-part mission—to provide consumer information and advocate for consumer privacy. The group raises awareness of how technology affects personal privacy, empowers consumers to take action to control their own personal information by providing practical tips on privacy protection, responds to privacy-related complaints from consumers, and reports this information. Its Web site provides transcripts of PRC speeches and testimony, stories of consumer experiences, and numerous fact sheets, including "Protecting Financial Privacy."

Bibliography

Books

Michael Chesbro   *Privacy Handbook: Proven Countermeasures for Combating Threats to Privacy, Security, and Personal Freedom.* Boulder, CO: Paladin Press, 2002.

Amitai Etzioni   *The Limits of Privacy.* New York: Basic Books, 2000.

Lawrence Friedman   *Guarding Life's Dark Secrets: Legal and Social Controls over Reputation, Propriety, and Privacy.* Palo Alto, CA: Stanford University Press, 2007.

Grant Hall   *Privacy Crisis: Identity Theft Prevention Plan and Guide to Anonymous Living.* Dublin, Ireland: James Clark King, 2006.

David H. Holtzman   *Privacy Lost: How Technology Is Endangering Your Privacy.* Hoboken, NJ: Jossey-Bass, 2006.

Caroline Kennedy and Ellen Alderman   *The Right of Privacy.* New York: Vintage, 1997.

Duncan Long	*Protect Your Privacy: How to Protect Your Identity as Well as Your Financial, Personal and Computer Records in an Age of Constant Surveillance.* Guildford, CT: Lyons, 2007.
Jon L. Mills	*Privacy: The Lost Right.* New York: Oxford University Press, 2008.
Kenneth W. Royce	*Bulletproof Privacy: How to Live Hidden, Happy and Free!* Gillette, WY: Javelin Press, 1997.
James B. Rule	*Privacy in Peril: How We Are Sacrificing a Fundamental Right in Exchange for Security and Convenience.* New York: Oxford University Press, 2009.
Wolfgang Sofsky	*Privacy: A Manifesto.* Princeton, NJ: Princeton University Press, 2008.
Daniel J. Solove	*The Digital Person: Technology and Privacy in the Information Age.* New York: New York University Press, 2006.
Daniel J. Solove	*The Future of Reputation: Gossip, Rumor, and Privacy on the Internet.* New Haven, CT: Yale University Press, 2008.
Daniel J. Solove	*Understanding Privacy.* Cambridge, MA: Harvard University Press, 2009.
John T. Soma and Stephen D. Rynerson	*Privacy Law in a Nutshell.* Eagan, MN: West, 2008.

B. Wilson   *Cover Your Tracks Without Changing Your Identity: How to Disappear Until You Want to Be Found.* Boulder, CO: Paladin Press, 2003.

Periodicals

Jill R. Aitoro   "Privacy, Security Must Be Key for FDA Drug-Tracking System," NextGov.com, June 2, 2009.

Jennifer Allen   "Don't Ask, Don't Tell," *Utne Reader,* November-December 2007.

Brian Bethune   "You Buy a Book but Don't Own It?" *Maclean's,* August 17, 2009.

Bob Brewin   "Cyber Criminals Overseas Steal U.S. Electronic Health Records," NextGov.com, August 11, 2009.

Lou Dobbs   "Is Nothing Private Anymore?" *U.S. News & World Report,* May 17, 2004.

Jessica Dye   "Article 55: Consumer Privacy Advocates Seek Search Engine Solution," *TecTrends Reporter,* May 2009.

John Fine   "Is an Online-Ad Crackdown Coming?" *BusinessWeek,* July 13, 2009.

Eric Goldman   "On the Mind: The Privacy Hoax," *Forbes,* October 14, 2002.

Shane Harris   "Precession and Privacy," NextGov.com, August 11, 2009.

Becky Hogge   "The Database Tyranny," *New Statesman*, May 4, 2009.

Paul Humphreys   "A Short Skirt, the Internet and Anonymity," *Psychology Review*, September 2009.

Dave Johnson   "Protect Your Privacy When Uploading Photos," *PC World*, July 2009.

Garret Keizer   "Notebook: Requiem for the Private Word," *Harper's Magazine*, August 2008.

Jill Rachlin   "Lessons in Privacy," *U.S. News & Marbaix   World Report*, September 6, 2004.

Susan McDonald   "Privacy—Headache or Non-Event?" *Business First-Louisville*, October 26, 2001.

Gautham Nagesh   "Passport System Breach Shows Privacy Practice Shortcomings," NextGov.com, August 11, 2009.

Zach Needles   "School Employees' Addresses Exempt from Right-to-Know Law," *Legal Intelligencer*, August 31, 2009.

Greg R. Notess   "Privacy in the Age of the Social Web," *Online*, July–August 2009.

J.R. Raphael   "People Search Engines: They Know Your Dark Secrets . . . and Tell Anyone," *PC World*, March 10, 2009.

Amy Lynn Sorrell "Doctors Prepare for ID Theft Rules," *American Medical News*, May 18, 2009.

William J. Stuntz "Secret Service—Against Privacy and Transparency," *New Republic*, April 17, 2006.

Index

A

Abortions, 8
Adams, Drew, 88–90
Advertising and marketing, 32, 36–37
Afghanistan, 61, 62
American Bar Association, 26
American Civil Liberties Union (ACLU)
    Colorado, 86–92
    employee privacy rights, 51, 54
    Technology and Liberty Project, 51
    See also New York Civil Liberties Union (NYCLU)
American Management Association (AMA), 49, 56
Anelay of St. Johns, Baroness, 42
Apple Computer, 83
Apple Valley High School (MN), 82–83
Armstrong High School (MN), 82

B

Bell, Sean, 20
Best Practices for the Protection of Personally Identifiable Information Associated with State Implementation of the REAL ID Act (DHS Privacy Office), 46
Blackmail, 41
Blogging, 31, 57
Bloomberg, Michael, 16
Boulder Valley School District (BVSD), 86–92

Branigan, Cara, 81–85
Bush, George W., 23
Buzznet.com, 83

C

Cell phones
    cell phone cameras, 81–85
    schools and, 86–92
    See also Telephones
Cellular Telecommunications and Internet Association, 84
Cheers (television program), 34
Children. *See* Minor's rights
China, 39
Class-action lawsuits, 14
Columbine High School shooting (CO), 82
Company cars, 52
Consumer authentication, 28
Contraception, 8
Courier-Journal (Louisville), 84
Crane, Amy B., 48–55
Crime deterrence, 21, 24

D

Dahl, David, 82
Databases
    Internet data mining, 30–33, 41–42
    misuse, 13, 24
    security, 28
DeWine, Mike, 84
Digital shoplifting, 84
Do-not-call registry, 35
Driver's license information, 13
Driver's Privacy Protection Act, 46

State Homeland Security Grant, 47
Stenhouse, Sue, 84

T

Tarver, Steve, 84
Telephones
 cell phone cameras, 81–85
 employer monitoring, 49, 51–52, 57
 schools and cell phones, 86–92
Tenth Circuit Court of Appeals, 74
Termination of employees, 50, 55, 57
Terrorism
 anti-terrorism, 20
 funding grants and, 47
 national ID cards and, 38
 privacy rights and, 42
 surveillance cameras and, 10, 11, 14
Turkey, 39
Twitter, 31, 33, 77

U

Union employees, 55
United Kingdom, 39, 41
U.S. Constitution, 13–15, 65–68, 73–75
U.S. Department of Defense, 64, 70–71
U.S. Department of Homeland Security, 43–47

U.S. Department of Transportation, 12
U.S. Government Accountability Office, 63
U.S. Office of Management and Budgets, 25
U.S. Postal Service, 25
U.S. Supreme Court, 8, 65, 74, 75

V

Video surveillance
 abuse, 17–22
 benefits, 18–19
 camera capabilities, 12
 cell phones, 81–85
 crime deterrence and, 21
 distribution of images, 11, 12–13
 employee monitoring, 51, 57, 59
 funding for, 20
 New York City and, 10–16
 required surveillance, 21–22
 United Kingdom, 41
 video archives, 11
Video Voyeurism Prevention Act of 2003, 84

W

Wheeler, Julie, 89
Workplace Fairness, 56, 57

Y

YMCA (KY), 84

CPSIA information can be obtained
at www.ICGtesting.com
Printed in the USA
FFOW03n0303200315
12018FF